THE DEATH AND RESURRECTION OF JESUS

JOHN PAUL HEIL

THE DEATH AND RESURRECTION OF JESUS

A Narrative–Critical Reading of Matthew 26–28

FORTRESS PRESS MINNEAPOLIS

THE DEATH AND RESURRECTION OF JESUS
A Narrative-Critical Reading of Matthew 26–28

All Scripture quotations are the author's translation.

Cover design: Patricia Boman
Cover art: Rembrandt van Rijn (1606–1669) *The Three Crosses*, 1653. Courtesy of Collection Museum Het Rembrandthuis, Amsterdam.
Interior design: Karen Buck
Composition: Polebridge Press

Library of Congress Cataloging-in-Publication Data

Heil, John Paul.
The death and resurrection of Jesus : a narrative-critical reading of Matthew 26–28 / John Paul Heil.
p. cm.
Includes bibliographical references and index.
ISBN 0-8006-2514-5 (alk. paper)
1. Bible. N.T. Matthew XXVI–XXVIII—Criticism. Narrative.
I. Title.
BS2575.2.H37 1991
226.2′066—dc20 91-30492
CIP

The paper used in this publication meets the minimum requirements of American National Standard for Information Sciences—Permanence of Paper for Printed Library Materials, ANSI Z329.48–1984. ∞™

Manufactured in the U.S.A. AF 1-2514

95 94 93 92 91 1 2 3 4 5 6 7 8 9 10

Contents

Abbreviations

AnBib	Analecta biblica
BAGD	W. Bauer, W. F. Arndt, F. W. Gingrich, and F. W. Danker, *Greek-English Lexicon of the NT*
BeO	*Bibbia e oriente*
BETL	Bibliotheca ephemeridum theologicarum lovaniensium
Bijdr	*Bijdragen*
BR	*Biblical Research*
BTB	*Biblical Theology Bulletin*
CBQ	*Catholic Biblical Quarterly*
CBQMS	Catholic Biblical Quarterly—Monograph Series
ConBNT	Coniectanea biblica, New Testament
ETL	*Ephemerides theologicae lovanienses*
HeyJ	*Heythrop Journal*
HTKNT	Herders theologischer Kommentar zum Neuen Testament
IBS	*Irish Biblical Studies*
ICC	International Critical Commentary
Int	*Interpretation*
JAAR	*Journal of the American Academy of Religion*
JBL	*Journal of Biblical Literature*
JSNT	*Journal for the Study of the New Testament*
JSNTSup	Journal for the Study of the New Testament—Supplement Series
JTS	*Journal of Theological Studies*
Neot	*Neotestamentica*
NovT	*Novum Testamentum*
NovTSup	Novum Testamentum, Supplements
NTS	*New Testament Studies*
OBO	Orbis biblicus et orientalis
QD	Quaestiones disputatae
RB	*Revue biblique*
RNT	Regensburger Neues Testament

RSR	*Recherches de science religieuse*
SBB	Stuttgarter biblische Beiträge
SBLASP	Society of Biblical Literature Abstracts and Seminar Papers
SBLDS	Society of Biblical Literature Dissertation Series
SBS	Stuttgarter Bibelstudien
SUNT	Studien zur Umwelt des Neuen Testaments
TDNT	*Theological Dictionary of the New Testament*
WUNT	Wissenschaftliche Untersuchungen zum Neuen Testament
ZNW	*Zeitschrift für die neutestamentliche Wissenschaft*

Preface

This book is the fruit of several years of interest and study of the literary and rhetorical aspects of the New Testament, more specifically of narrative criticism with an emphasis on reader response, that is, the effect the text has on its implied reader. Throughout my years of study and teaching of the New Testament, I have always been amazed by the many purposeful and precise literary patterns it contains and how they effectively communicate the author's message. The pages that follow here are intended to demonstrate the intricate and dynamic design that I have discovered in Matthew's narrative of the passion, death, and resurrection of Jesus and how it can deepen our appreciation of the message communicated by the last chapters of the Matthean Gospel.

Every author is dependent on the work and encouragement of others. I am grateful for the insights I have gained from the authors I have read, as well as from my teachers and students over the years. I particularly appreciate the inspiration I have received as a member of the Catholic Biblical Association Task Force on the Narrative Study of the New Testament.

I hope this book will help Christian preachers, teachers, and students to understand better the depth and richness of the events of Jesus' death and resurrection as recorded by Matthew, a scribe instructed in the kingdom of heaven (Matt 13:52), so that we may all fulfill the great commission of the Matthean risen Jesus to go and make disciples of all nations by "teaching them to observe all that I have commanded you" (Matt 28:19–20).

CHAPTER 1

Introduction

Narrative Criticism and Reader Response

In biblical studies narrative criticism has emerged as an illuminating way to reveal the richness of the Gospel narratives as artistic, literary communications. In what follows we shall apply the method of narrative criticism to the account of the passion, death, and resurrection of Jesus in the Gospel of Matthew, chapters 26–28, with a special emphasis on the responses of the implied reader. Through this narrative-critical, reader-response approach, we intend to provide a new illustration of how these Gospel stories operate as a dynamic process of communication.

By "implied reader" we mean the reader or audience that the text presupposes. Not real or historical, the implied reader is a theoretical construct that represents the responses that the implied author intends or assumes on the part of his audience. Every text presupposes a reader/hearer/audience in order to be actualized as an act of communication; it is "the reader" anticipated and created by the text in the process of reading or listening to it.[1]

In accord with our reader-response approach, we are concerned with the "rhetorical effect" the text produces for its implied reader.[2] We focus upon the responses of the implied reader as determined by the various presuppositions, strategies, codes, and indicators within Matthew's narrative.[3] More specifically we examine what the alternating and progressive sequence of contrasting scenes in Matthew 26–28 does to its reader or audience and how it affects that reader, that is, what the dynamic narrative structure of Matthew 26–28 causes its reader to experience in order to uncover and produce the meaning latent in the text and thus to bring its act of communication to completion.[4] The result is a demonstration of how the reader is to respond to and interpret the total progression of events involved in the Matthean presentation of Jesus' passion, death, and resurrection.

Narrative Structure of Matthew 26–28

The intriguing narrative structure of Matthew 26–28 divides itself into three main sections, Matt 26:1–56, 26:57—27:54 and 27:55—28:20, each composed of nine scenes that function together as a dynamic progression of seven narrative intercalations or "sandwiches." In other words, each main section of nine scenes progresses as an interchanging sequence of seven a-b-a or b-a-b narrative sandwiches. The following is an outline of the three main divisions, illustrating their respective sequence of scenes.

Narrative Structure of the Passion, Death, and Resurrection of Jesus in Matthew 26–28

I. Matt 26:1–56: Jesus prepares for and accepts his death.
- (1) 26:1–16: Jesus anticipates his death by Jewish leaders.
  - a^1 26:1–5: Jewish leaders plot the arrest and death of Jesus.
  - b^1 26:6–13: The death of Jesus is anticipated during a meal.
  - a^2 26:14–16: A disciple plans to betray Jesus to death.
- (2) 26:17–29: Jesus prepares his disciples for his death.
  - b^2 26:17–19: Jesus directs his disciples to prepare the Passover meal.
  - a^3 26:20–25: During the meal Jesus predicts betrayal by the disciple Judas.
  - b^3 26:26–29: Through the Passover Meal Jesus and his disciples share in his triumph over death.
- (3) 26:30–56: Jesus accepts death through prayer.
  - a^4 26:30–35: Jesus predicts abandonment/denial by his disciples.
  - b^4 26:36–46: While still with his disciples Jesus accepts death through prayer.
  - a^5 26:47–56: Jesus is arrested, betrayed by Judas, and abandoned by his disciples.

II. Matt 26:57—27:54: The innocent Jesus dies as true King and Son of God.
- (1) 26:57–75: Jesus admits his divine sonship.
  - a^1 26:57–58: Peter follows while Jesus is led to the high priest.
  - b^1 26:59–68: Jesus admits his divine sonship to the high priest and is condemned to death.
  - a^2 26:69–75: Peter denies Jesus in the courtyard of the high priest.
- (2) 27:1–14: The innocent Jesus admits his kingship.
  - b^2 27:1–2: The condemned but innocent Jesus is led to Pilate.
  - a^3 27:3–10: Judas repents because of Jesus' innocence.
  - b^3 27:11–14: The innocent Jesus admits his kingship to Pilate.
- (3) 27:15–54: Jesus dies as God's innocent, royal Son.
  - a^4 27:15–26: Jewish people accept guilt for the death of the innocent Jesus.

b^4 27:27–44: While dying, the innocent Jesus is mocked as King and Son of God.

a^5 27:45–54: The death of the innocent Jesus vindicates his divine sonship.

III. Matt 27:55—28:20: The authority of the risen Jesus prevails through witnesses of his death, burial, and resurrection.

(1) 27:55–61: Women followers witness Jesus' death and burial.

a^1 27:55–56: Women followers from Galilee witness the death of Jesus.

b^1 27:57–60: A rich disciple from Arimathea receives the body of Jesus from Pilate, buries it in his own tomb, rolls the stone, and departs.

a^2 27:61: Mary Magdalene and the other Mary sit facing the tomb of Jesus.

(2) 27:62—28:4: Jewish leaders try to thwart Jesus' resurrection.

b^2 27:62–66: Chief priests and Pharisees receive Pilate's permission to seal the stone and guard the tomb.

a^3 28:1: Mary Magdalene and the other Mary go to see the tomb.

b^3 28:2–4: An angel rolls back the stone, and the fearful guards become as if dead.

(3) 28:5–20: The authority of the risen Jesus prevails.

a^4 28:5–10: The women are sent to the disciples by the angel and the risen Jesus.

b^4 28:11–15: The chief priests and elders bribe the guards to say that the disciples stole the body of Jesus.

a^5 28:16–20: In Galilee the eleven disciples see the risen Jesus and are sent to make disciples of all peoples.

In each of these three major sections of Matthew 26–28, the nine scenes progress in a dynamically alternating sequence forming seven sets of narrative sandwiches, as illustrated in the following tables:

I. Matt 26:1–56: Jesus prepares for and accepts his death.

Nine Scenes		1. Jewish leaders plot arrest and death of Jesus.	2. Death of Jesus is anticipated during a meal.	3. A disciple plans to betray Jesus to death.	4. Jesus directs disciples to prepare Passover meal.	5. During meal Jesus predicts betrayal by disciple Judas.	6. Jesus and his disciples share his triumph over death in Passover meal.	7. Jesus predicts abandonment and denial by disciples.	8. While still with disciples Jesus accepts death through prayer.	9. Jesus is arrested, betrayed by Judas, and abandoned by disciples.
Seven	(1)	a^1 26:1-5	b^1 26:6-13	a^2 26:14-16						
Narrative Sandwiches	(2)		b^1 26:6-13	a^2 26:14-16	b^2 26:17-19					
	(3)			a^2 26:14-16	b^2 26:17-19	a^3 26:20-25				
	(4)				b^2 26:17-19	a^3 26:20-25	b^3 26:26-29			
	(5)					a^3 26:20-25	b^3 26:26-29	a^4 26:30-35		
	(6)						b^3 26:26-29	a^4 26:30-35	b^4 26:36-46	
	(7)							a^4 26:30-35	b^4 26:36-46	a^5 26:47-56

Note that where overlapping or sandwiching occurs (26:14–16, 26:17–19, etc.), such scenes are pivotal to the narrative structure. They form a literary progression with other scenes eliciting a similar audience response (a^1, a^2, a^3, a^4, a^5) and also create a tension with scenes eliciting a different audience response (b^1, b^2, b^3, b^4).

In Matt 26:1–56 the reader experiences opposition and separation from Jesus in the progression of a scenes in contrast to close union with Jesus in the progression of b scenes.

II. Matt 26:57—27:54: The innocent Jesus dies as true King and Son of God.

Nine Scenes		1. Peter follows while Jesus is led to high priest.	2. Jesus admits his divine sonship to high priest and is condemned to death.	3. Peter denies Jesus in courtyard of high priest.	4. The condemned but innocent Jesus is led to Pilate.	5. Judas repents because of Jesus' innocence.	6. The innocent Jesus admits his kingship to Pilate.	7. Jewish people accept guilt for death of the innocent Jesus.	8. While dying the innocent Jesus is mocked as King and Son of God.	9. The death of the innocent Jesus vindicates his divine sonship.
Seven	(1)	a^1 26:57-58	b^1 26:59-68	a^2 26:69-75						
Narrative Sandwiches	(2)		b^1 26:59-68	a^2 26:69-75	b^2 27:1-2					
	(3)			a^2 26:69-75	b^2 27:1-2	a^3 27:3-10				
	(4)				b^2 27:1-2	a^3 27:3-10	b^3 27:11-14			
	(5)					a^3 27:3-10	b^3 27:11-14	a^4 27:15-26		
	(6)						b^3 27:11-14	a^4 27:15-26	b^4 27:27-44	
	(7)							a^4 27:15-26	b^4 27:27-44	a^5 27:45-54

In Matt 26:57—27:54 the reader experiences the Jewish leaders ironically establishing Jesus as the messianic King and Son of God by putting him to an unjust death in the b scenes in contrast to those who confirm the innocence and profound identity of Jesus by withdrawing from his unjust death in the a scenes.

In Matt 27:55—28:20 the reader experiences reliable witnesses from the death to the resurrection of Jesus, culminating in authentic faith in and empowerment by the risen Lord in the a scenes in contrast to the futile and fraudulent attempts to prevent faith in the risen Jesus in the b scenes.

III. Matt 27:55—28:20: The authority of the risen Jesus prevails through witnesses of his death, burial, and resurrection.

Nine Scenes		1. Women followers from Galilee witness the death of Jesus.	2. A rich disciple receives the body of Jesus from Pilate, buries it, rolls the stone, and departs.	3. Mary Magdalene and the other Mary sit facing the tomb of Jesus.	4. Chief priests and Pharisees receive Pilate's permission to seal the stone and guard the tomb.	5. Mary Magdalene and the other Mary go to see the tomb.	6. An angel rolls back the stone, and the fearful guards become as if dead.	7. The women are sent to the disciples by the angel and the risen Jesus.	8. Chief priests and elders bribe the guards to say that the disciples stole the body of Jesus.	9. In Galilee the eleven disciples see the risen Jesus and are sent to make disciples of all peoples.
Seven	(1)	a^1 27:55–56	b^1 27:57–60	a^2 27:61						
Narrative Sandwiches	(2)		b^1 27:57–60	a^2 27:61	b^2 27:62–66					
	(3)			a^2 27:61	b^2 27:62–66	a^3 28:1				
	(4)				b^2 27:62–66	a^3 28:1	b^3 28:2–4			
	(5)					a^3 28:1	b^3 28:2–4	a^4 28:5–10		
	(6)						b^3 28:2–4	a^4 28:5–10	b^4 28:11–15	
	(7)							a^4 28:5–10	b^4 28:11–15	a^5 28:16–20

In the next three chapters of our investigation we will be concerned with how this narrative structure evokes and affects the responses of the Matthean reader to the events of Jesus' passion, death, and resurrection. As we will see, major themes are developed and contrasted for the reader by means of the alternations of continually contrasting scenes, in which each successive scene is contrastingly framed or sandwiched by two other mutually related scenes. But first we want to consider how the preceding narrative prepares the reader for the experience of the final chapters.

The Previous Narrative Prepares for Matthew 26–28

Infancy Narrative (Matthew 1–2)

Jesus as the Christ. The Matthean narrative begins with the announcement "The book of the origin of Jesus Christ, Son of David, Son of Abraham" (1:1). The genealogy that follows (1:2–16) assures the reader that this "Jesus who is called Christ" (1:16) is "the Christ," the long-awaited messiah or "one anointed" by God as his definitive agent for the salvation of Israel, because his birth occurs as the summit of Israel's salvation history. Jesus' genealogy demonstrates that he is truly "the Christ" since his origin can be traced through the fourteen generations from Abraham to David (a high point), through the fourteen generations from David to the Babylonian exile (a low point), through the fourteen generations from the Babylonian exile until the climax of Israel's salvation history with the birth of Jesus as "the Christ" (1:17). The place of Jesus' birth in "Bethlehem of Judea" (2:1) in accord with God's scriptural plan (2:5–6) further assures the reader that Jesus has the credentials to be called "the Christ" (2:4), the ruler who was expected to shepherd God's people Israel (2:6).

In his ministry to Israel Jesus indicates that he is "the Christ" by performing "the works of the Christ" (11:2), his miraculous healings and preaching of the gospel (11:5). Although Peter confesses that Jesus is "the Christ, the Son of the living God" (16:16), Jesus orders his disciples to tell no one that he is "the Christ" (16:20), hinting that there is more to be revealed about his identity and character as the Christ. Jesus later reveals that "the Christ" (22:42) is not only the "son" but also the "lord" of David (22:42–45), that "the Christ" is the only one who should be called "master" (23:10), and that before his final coming false christs will arise to deceive many by claiming to be "the Christ" (24:5, 23).

The issue of Jesus as the Christ comes to a head at his trial in the passion narrative. After the high priest places him under oath before the "living God," Jesus openly admits that he is "the Christ, the Son of God" (26:63–64). He is then judged deserving of death and brutally mocked as a prophesying "Christ" (26:66–68). When Pilate offers to release the prisoner Barabbas or "Jesus who is called Christ" (27:17, 22), the crowd chooses the notorious Barabbas and demands that the innocent Jesus be crucified (27:21–23). With the words "his blood be upon us and our children," the "whole people" of Israel accepts full responsibility for the death of the innocent Jesus, their true Christ (27:25). The reader experiences the terrible tragedy that the "Jesus who is called Christ" because his birth marks the summit of Israel's salvation history (1:16) is ruthlessly rejected by his own people precisely as the "Jesus who is called Christ" (27:17, 22).

Jesus as Savior. When the angel of the Lord informs the troubled Joseph that it is through the Holy Spirit that Mary has conceived a child, he instructs Joseph to accept Mary as his wife and to name the child "Jesus" because "he will save his people from their sins" (1:20–21). The need for the people of Jesus to be "saved" from their "sins" becomes evident as crowds from Jerusalem, all Judea, and the whole region around the Jordan River came to receive John's baptism of repentance, "confessing their sins" (3:5–6). Through Jesus' miraculous healings and exorcisms, which are personal experiences of the salvation he is bringing about for his people,[5] he begins to fulfill his role as the one who "will save his people from their sins." When Jesus heals the paralytic (9:1–8), for example, he demonstrates that his healing includes the forgiveness of sins (9:2, 5) and reveals that he, as the Son of Man, has heavenly authority to forgive sins on earth (9:6). This prepares the reader for the climax of the theme of Jesus as savior from sins when he symbolically interprets the wine of his final Passover meal as "my blood of the covenant, which will be shed on behalf of many for the forgiveness of sins" (26:28). It is by his death, then, that Jesus finally completes his role as the one who "will save his people from their sins."

While he is dying on the cross, Jesus' ability to be a "savior" is ironically mocked by the very people whose salvation his death is effecting. Passers-by taunt him to "save" himself by coming down from the cross (27:39–40). The Jewish leadership, the chief priests with the scribes and elders, revile him as one who "saved" others but cannot "save" himself by coming down from the cross (27:41–42). That Jesus "saved" others recalls how he healed people such as the woman with a hemorrhage whose faith cured or "saved" her (9:20–22), and how he "saved" his disciples from death in sea storms (8:25; 14:30). As Jesus utters his death cry, bystanders wonder whether Elijah might come to "save" him (27:49). But God's raising of Jesus from the dead (27:51–53) vindicates him as savior of his people precisely by refusing to "save" himself. By dying in faithful subordination to God's will, Jesus personally authenticates his teaching that salvation comes from God, who will ultimately "save" those who entrust themselves completely to him (19:25–26; 24:22). Jesus' death and resurrection confirm for the reader the validity of his instructions to his disciples that whoever wishes to "save" his life will lose it (16:25) and whoever perseveres to the end "will be saved" (10:22; 24:13). His resurrection after dying with faith in God proves that he truly is what his name "Jesus" signifies, the savior who "will save his people from their sins."

Jesus as God-With-Us. The infancy narrative continues with the narrator's notice that "they," that is, the people whom Jesus will save from their sins (1:21), "will call his name Emmanuel, which means 'God is with us'" in fulfillment of what the Lord said through the prophet (Isa 7:14; 8:8 in 1:23). Jesus illustrates how he represents God's special saving presence with his people not only through his teaching and healing ministry but also by his pledge for the prayer gatherings of his followers: "Where two or three are gathered together in my name, there am I in the midst of them" (18:20). In the last line of the Gospel the powerful, reassuring promise of the risen Jesus to his disciples climaxes his role as "God-With-Us" by extending his definitive salvific presence to the time of the reader and beyond: "And behold, I am with you all days until the end of the age" (28:20).

Jesus as the true King. Closely related to the theme of Jesus as the Christ is that of Jesus as the king of the Jews. Jesus is a royal descendant of David "the king" (1:6), who marks the first high point of the salvation historical genealogy climaxed by the birth of Jesus as the Christ (1:16–17). After the gentile magi from the East arrive in Jerusalem and ask Herod, the reigning "king," where the newborn "king of the Jews" is, "King" Herod and all Jerusalem with him become troubled (2:1–3). When Herod then inquires of the chief priests and scribes where "the Christ" is to be born, they tell him, "in Bethlehem of Judea" (2:4–5), precisely where Jesus has been born (2:1). The birth of Jesus "in Bethlehem of Judea" indicates that he is the expected "ruler" who would emerge from the land of Judea, the true shepherd-king who would "shepherd" God's entire people of Israel in fulfillment of the prophecy of the Jewish Scriptures (Mic 5:1; 2 Sam 5:2), as quoted by the chief priests and scribes (2:5–6). After the magi extend to the newborn Jesus the worship befitting him as a "king," they are divinely guided to return not to King Herod but to their own country (2:11–12).

That Jesus functions as the true shepherd-king of Israel becomes evident in 9:36 as he feels compassion for the crowds because they were troubled and abandoned, "like sheep without a shepherd" (Num 27:17; 1 Kgs 22:17). He then sends out his twelve disciples with power to continue his healing ministry (10:1) toward these "lost sheep of the house of Israel" (10:6; see also 15:24). The deep "compassion" (9:36; 14:14; 15:32) of Jesus for the shepherdless crowds following him prompts him to demonstrate how he is the true shepherd-king of Israel (Ezekiel 34) by gathering them together and overabundantly feeding them (14:13–21; 15:32–38). Jesus thus shows that he is a true king of his people in contrast to the tetrarch Herod Antipas, who proves himself to be a false "king" (14:9), pathetically manipulated by his adultery to murder the revered prophet John the Baptist (14:3–12).

When Jesus enters Jerusalem as the meek "king" of Israel in fulfillment of scriptural prophecy (Zech 9:9 in 21:5), "the whole city" is shaken as they query his identity (21:10), reminding the reader of how "all Jerusalem" had earlier become agitated when the magi inquired about the newborn "king" of the Jews (2:2–3). And in the closing scene of the last of the five major discourses of Jesus in Matthew, Jesus implicitly refers to himself as the "king" (25:34) who will execute the final judgment.

But the theme of Jesus as the true "king" attains its culmination in the passion narrative. Interrogated by the gentile governor Pilate, Jesus admits that he is "the king of the Jews" (27:11). Although Pilate extricates himself from the guilt of crucifying the innocent Jesus (27:24), his soldiers derisively hail him as "the king of the Jews" (27:29). This abusive mock investiture of Jesus as the king of the Jews by gentile soldiers (27:27–31) keenly contrasts the reverent worship of him as king of the Jews by the gentile magi in the infancy narrative (2:11–12).

By insulting the innocent Jesus (27:30), the soldiers ironically reveal the profound, paradoxical nature of his kingship; namely, that he is the true "king of the Jews" precisely because he obediently endures violent humiliation as the suffering servant of God (Isa 50:6). Their crucifixion of him in a mock royal enthronement with a criminal on his right and on his left (27:38) continues to establish him as God's "suffering servant" (Isa 53:12), who undergoes an unjust death in order to become exactly what their ridiculing charge over his head announces: "This is Jesus, the King of the Jews" (27:37). Although Jesus fulfills the prophecy for a king who would "shepherd my people Israel" (2:6) as uttered in the infancy narrative by "all the chief priests and scribes of the people" (2:4), the "chief priests with the scribes and elders" (27:41) climax the mockery of his kingship as they taunt him to come down from the cross to prove he is "the king of Israel" (27:42). The reader experiences the tragic irony that it is precisely by dying on the cross as the scorned king of his people that Jesus becomes the true "king of Israel."

Jesus as the Son of God. The theme of Jesus as the unique Son of God begins in the infancy narrative as Jesus relives Israel's experience of God's salvation from Egypt in the exodus. To escape the murderous threat of Herod, Joseph is divinely directed to take the child and his mother to Egypt (2:13–14). When they return after Herod's death, the prophetic word of God is fulfilled that states, "Out of Egypt I have called my son" (Hos 11:1 in 2:15). Like Israel in the exodus (Exod 4:22), Jesus is designated God's own Son who experiences God's rescue from death (2:16–18) by being called out of Egypt.

When Jesus is endowed with the Spirit of God after his baptism (3:16), God's heavenly voice explicitly reinforces Jesus' divine sonship with the proclamation, "This is my beloved Son, with whom I am well pleased" (3:17). Although the devil pointedly tests this divine sonship of Jesus with the words "if you are the Son of God" (4:3, 6), Jesus proves that he is indeed God's Son by not succumbing to his tempter's taunts but by admirably remaining obedient to the scriptural word of God (4:1–11). And the Gadarene demons' knowledge of Jesus as "Son of God" (8:29) cannot prevent Jesus from destroying them (8:32).

After Jesus thanks his heavenly Father for giving him the power to uniquely know the Father as "the Son" who can reveal the Father to whomever he wishes (11:25–27), Jesus reveals to his disciples his absolute divine power to save them by walking across the sea (14:22–32), so that they worship him, confessing, "Truly, you are the Son of God!" (14:33). Peter later reinforces this by confessing, "You are the Christ, the Son of the living God!" (16:16). At Jesus' transfiguration (17:1–8) God's heavenly pronouncement that "this is my beloved Son, with whom I am well pleased" (17:5) not only reaffirms his previous proclamation of Jesus' divine sonship (3:17), but his additional words, "listen to him," direct the privileged disciples to pay attention to Jesus' predictions of the divine necessity of his passion, death and resurrection (16:21; 17:22–23; 20:17–19). In his parable about the wicked tenants (21:33–46) Jesus indirectly indicts the Jewish authorities in Jerusalem (21:45–46) as those who will murder him as "the Son" (22:37–38) of God.

All of this prepares the reader for the climax of the theme of Jesus' divine sonship in the passion narrative. After Jesus confirms his divine sonship through his Gethsemane prayer (26:36–46) of obedience to the will of "my Father" (26:39, 42) that he suffer and die, he openly admits to the high priest under oath before the living God that he is the Christ, "the Son of God" (26:63–64), which results in his condemnation to death (26:66). Jesus' confession that he is the Son of God is then mocked by those passing by at his crucifixion. With a taunt reminiscent of the devil's tactics to test his divine sonship (4:3, 6), they goad him to save himself, "if you are the Son of God," by coming down from the cross (27:39–40). Then the chief priests with the scribes and elders bring this final test of Jesus' divine sonship to its apex by scoffing, "He trusted in God; let him rescue him now if he wants him. For he said, 'I am the Son of God'" (27:43). The Jewish authorities' jeering for God to "rescue him now if he wants him" recalls God's earlier rescue of Jesus in the infancy narrative as "his Son" from murder by Herod (2:13–15).

But Jesus' death as the Son of God in obedience to his Father's will is dramatically vindicated by God himself. The God who had earlier rescued Jesus by calling him out of Egypt as "my Son" (2:15) now rescues him after he has died by raising him from the dead, thus inaugurating the definitive salvation of his people (27:51–53). In triumphant contrast to the Jewish leaders' scorn of Jesus' divine sonship (27:43), the gentile centurion and those with him climactically confirm God's vindication of it by proclaiming, "Truly, this was the Son of God!" (27:54). Finally, the risen Jesus himself affirms his abiding divine sonship as he commissions his disciples to make disciples of all nations by baptizing them "in the name of the Father, and of the Son, and of the Holy Spirit" (28:19).

Jesus as the Nazorean from Galilee. The infancy narrative initiates a geographical theme of opposition between Nazareth and Galilee on the one hand and Jerusalem and Judea on the other. When Joseph returns from Egypt with the child Jesus and his mother, he settles in the region of Galilee rather than in the ominous region of Judea, now ruled by Archelaus, the son of the murderous Herod (2:19–22). That Jesus dwells in the city of Nazareth fulfills the scriptural prophecy that "he shall be called a Nazorean" (2:23), indicating that he is a specially consecrated agent of God's salvation (Judg 13:5, 7; 16:17; Isa 4:3; 11:1). The city of Jerusalem, as the dangerous origin of Herod's menacing scheme (2:1–3), and the risky region of Judea begin to emerge for the reader as perilous places of Jewish opposition to Jesus in contrast to the prophetically significant city of Nazareth and the safe region of Galilee.

Although Jesus leaves Galilee to be baptized by John (3:13) and endure satanic temptations in the wilderness (4:1–11), after John is arrested, he returns to Galilee (4:12). His leaving of Nazareth to dwell in Capernaum in the Galilean districts of Zebulun and Naphtali fulfills the Isaian prophecy (Isa 9:1–2) that refers to Galilee as "Galilee of the nations" (4:15), thus indicating Galilee's universalistic orientation. It is while walking by the Sea of Galilee that Jesus calls his first four followers (4:18–22). His teaching and healing ministry extends throughout "all of Galilee" (4:23) and draws many crowds not only from Galilee but beyond—from "Decapolis, Jerusalem, and Judea, and from beyond the Jordan" (4:25)—thus establishing Galilee as the prominent place of his ministry with an attraction toward "the nations." Although temporarily leaving Galilee for the region of Tyre and Sidon, where he heals the daughter of a Canaanite woman (15:21–28), Jesus promptly returns to Galilee to continue his healing ministry to the many crowds going to him there (15:29–31).

Jesus' predictions of his passion, death, and resurrection (16:21; 17:22–23; 20:17–19) develop the threatening nature of Jerusalem begun in the infancy narrative (2:1–3). It is in Jerusalem (16:21; 20:17–18) of Judea in contrast to Galilee, as the place where his disciples gather around him (17:22), that the Jewish leaders will perpetrate his death. But even when Jesus leaves Galilee to begin his fateful journey through the region of Judea beyond the Jordan, he continues to heal the many crowds following him (19:1–2). When Jesus majestically enters Jerusalem, the commotion of "the whole city" (21:10) reminds the reader of the earlier distress of "all Jerusalem" at the news of Jesus' birth (2:3). The crowds' announcement that "this is the prophet Jesus from Nazareth of Galilee" (21:11) not only ironically fulfills Jesus' proverbial prediction, when he was rejected by his own people at Nazareth (13:54–58), that "a prophet is not without honor except in his native place and in his own house" (13:57), but also establishes the contrast between Jesus as God's special "Nazorean" from Nazareth of Galilee (2:23) and the opposing Jewish leaders in Jerusalem of Judea.

The theme of these opposing geographical references comes to its climax in the passion narrative. After Jesus predicts that all of his disciples, who had earlier gathered around him in Galilee (17:22), will abandon him (26:31), he promises that after he has been raised up he "will go before you to Galilee" (26:32). When Peter denies Jesus (26:69–75), he renounces any association with Jesus as "the Galilean" (26:69) and as "the Nazorean" (26:71). Peter thereby repudiates not only his discipleship as one of the first four followers called by Jesus in Galilee (4:18–22) but also his affiliation with "the Nazorean," God's specially consecrated agent of salvation (2:23). Women followers from Galilee witness the death of Jesus as substitutes for the absent male disciples (27:55–56). They are sent by both the angel (28:7) and the risen Jesus to direct the disciples back to Galilee for their promised reunion (26:32) with Jesus as his "brothers" (28:10). When the eleven disciples return to Galilee (28:16) and see the risen Jesus, he commissions them to make disciples of "all nations" (28:19). This fittingly fulfills Galilee's prophetic role as "Galilee of the nations" (4:15) in contrast to Jerusalem of Judea, where a false story of Jesus' resurrection has circulated among the Jews to the present day (28:11–15).

John the Baptist

The passion and death of John the Baptist despite his being a prophet respected by the people prepares the reader for the similar fate of Jesus. The role played by the Baptist in the Matthean narrative prefigures, parallels, and complements that of Jesus. The keynote of the preaching of both is the same: "Repent, for the kingdom of heaven is at hand!" (3:2; 4:17). Whereas John draws people from "Jerusalem, all Judea, and the whole region around the Jordan" (3:5), Jesus attracts great crowds from "all of Syria . . . Galilee, the Decapolis, Jerusalem, and Judea, and from beyond the Jordan" (4:24–25). Both clash with the "Pharisees and Sadducees," who form a united front of opposition (3:7; 16:1–12). In their teaching both warn that "every tree that does not bear good fruit will be cut down and thrown into the fire" (3:10; 7:19). Just as John reproaches his opponents with the words "brood of vipers, who has shown you how to flee from the coming wrath?" (3:7), Jesus similarly rebukes his opponents: "Brood of vipers, how shall you flee the judgment of Gehenna?" (23:33; see also 12:34).[6]

Although John is reluctant to baptize Jesus because he recognizes the superiority of Jesus' own "baptism" with the "Holy Spirit and fire" (3:11–14), Jesus persuades him to do so in order that together they can fulfill "all righteousness," that is, God's plan of salvation (3:15). As the narrative unfolds they continue to play their parallel and complementary roles in carrying out God's salvific will. Once Jesus hears of John's arrest, he returns to Galilee not only to take up John's cause of announcing the imminent arrival of the kingdom of heaven (3:2; 4:17) but also to begin to make it a reality by calling followers, teaching, preaching, and healing (4:12–25). But that John has been "arrested" or "handed over" (*paredothē*, 4:12) foreshadows the same destiny that awaits Jesus in the passion narrative when he is "handed over" (*paradidotai*) or "betrayed" by Judas (26:14–16, 45–50), as he himself had predicted (17:22; 20:18; 26:2, 20–25).

Jesus points out that John is not only a prophet but "more than a prophet" (11:9); indeed, he plays the role of "Elijah" (11:14), the prophetic figure who was expected to come as God's "messenger" to "prepare your way before you" (Exod 23:20 and Mal 3:1 in 11:10), thus serving as the forerunner to God's final age of salvation. It is by dying as a prophet that John preeminently prepares the way for Jesus' salvific death. Herod has John put to death despite his fear of the people who regarded John as a prophet (14:5). Similarly the Jewish authorities have Jesus put to death despite their fear of the crowds who regarded Jesus as a prophet (21:11, 46; 26:4–5). John's burial by his disciples (14:12) is paralleled by Jesus' burial by his disciple, Joseph of Arimathea (27:57–60). After the death of John as the prophetic Elijah figure who "must come first" (17:10), Jesus forewarns his disciples that he will be treated similarly (17:12).

Although John came "in the way of righteousness" as a prophet revered by the people (21:26), the Jewish leaders did not repent and believe him (21:32). Indeed, Jesus castigates the scribes and Pharisees for continuing their ancestors' shedding of "the blood of the prophets" (23:30–32). Because they continually murder the prophets sent to them by God (23:34), they bring upon themselves the guilt of "all the righteous blood shed upon earth, from the righteous blood of Abel to the blood of Zechariah, the son of Barachiah" (23:35), a prophet (Zech 1:1). This piercing reprimand by Jesus receives a climactic demonstration in the passion narrative. Despite Judas's remorseful admission to the chief priests and elders that "I have sinned in betraying innocent blood" (27:4) and Pilate's disclaimer that "I am innocent of this man's blood" (27:24), the Jewish leaders persuade the crowds to accept the guilt for the innocent blood of the Jesus they regarded as a prophet (21:11, 46). The "whole people" said, "His blood be upon us and our children" (27:25). Both John and Jesus suffer the destiny of the many prophets murdered by their own people—John as the prophetic Elijah figure, who as the forerunner of Jesus is "more than a prophet" (11:9), and Jesus as the innocent one, who by dying as a rejected prophet proves to be the messianic King of Israel and Son of God.

Conflict with Jewish Authorities

The infancy narrative already foreshadows for the reader the conflict that Jesus will have with Jewish authorities. Herod, the reigning king of the Jews, tries with the help of the chief priests and scribes (2:4) to murder Jesus, the newborn king of the Jews (2:1–18). In the passion narrative, after the chief priests and the elders have contrived for Jesus to be crucified (26:3–4, 47, 57–67; 27:1, 12, 20), the chief priests with the scribes and elders mock the dying Jesus as the king of Israel (27:41–42). And the confrontation that John the Baptist, the forerunner of Jesus, has with the Pharisees and Sadducees (3:7–12) anticipates the controversies Jesus will have with the same two groups, who oppose him together (16:1–12) as well as separately (Pharisees in 9:11, 34; 12:2, 14, 24, 38; 15:1; 19:3; 21:45; 22:15, 34, 41; 23:2, 13–15, 26; Sadducees in 22:23).

The charge of blasphemy that the scribes raise against Jesus when he forgives the sins of a paralytic (9:3) culminates in the passion narrative at the trial of Jesus before the Sanhedrin, when, after Jesus admits his messianic divine sonship (26:63–64), the high priest exclaims, "He has blasphemed!" (26:65), for which he is condemned to death (26:66). The Jewish leaders' opposition to Jesus gradually grows as the Pharisees, who judge that Jesus drives out demons only by the power of Beelzebul, the prince of demons (9:34; 12:24), decide to put him to death, since he has healed on the Sabbath (12:9–14). They finally succeed in their attempt to arrest Jesus (21:45–46) and have him put to death (26:3–4) as Judas's betrayal enables them to arrest him (26:47–50); then they condemn him to death (26:57–66), lead him to Pilate to be put to death (27:1–2, 11–14), persuade the people to demand his crucifixion from a reluctant Pilate (27:15–26), and mock him whom they have put to death as the King of Israel and Son of God (27:41–43).

The temple of Jerusalem, the center of Jewish worship with its sanctuary of God's special presence, plays a prominent part in the conflict between Jesus and the Jewish authorities. After Jesus allows his disciples to satisfy their hunger on the Sabbath, to the dismay of the Pharisees (12:1–8), part of his explanation includes the proclamation that "something greater than the temple is here" (12:6). When Jesus enters the temple, he incites the indignation of the chief priests and scribes by condemning the Jewish leadership for transforming the temple as God's "house of prayer" into a "den of thieves," and by healing the blind and the lame (21:12–17), who were not permitted in the temple (2 Sam 5:8). One after another of the various groups comprising the entire Jewish leadership encounter the authority of Jesus in the temple: The chief priests and elders question his authority over the temple (21:23–27); the disciples of the Pharisees with the Herodians try to entrap him with the issue of paying taxes to Caesar (22:15–22); the Sadducees attempt to ridicule him with the issue of resurrection (22:23–33); a lawyer of the Pharisees tries to muzzle him with the question of the greatest commandment (22:34–40); but Jesus silences the Pharisees with his teaching about the Davidic sonship of the Christ (22:41–46), and denounces the leadership of the scribes and Pharisees (23:1–36). After Jesus leaves the temple, he predicts its destruction (24:1–2).

The theme of Jesus' power and authority over the temple achieves its apex at his death. During his trial before the Sanhedrin, Jesus is accused of having claimed, "I can destroy the sanctuary of God and within three days rebuild it" (26:61). At his crucifixion those passing by revile him, saying, "You who would destroy the sanctuary and in three days rebuild it, save yourself, if you are the Son of God, and come down from the cross!" (27:39–40). The action of God himself vindicates and demonstrates the truth of these claims for Jesus' power and authority over the temple. Once Jesus has died, "the veil of the sanctuary was torn in two from top to bottom" (27:51) by God (divine passive), presaging the temple's demise. And then, "the earth quaked, rocks were split, tombs were opened, and the bodies of many saints who had fallen asleep were raised. And coming forth from their tombs after his resurrection, they entered the holy city and appeared to many" (27:51b-53). God's dramatic raising of the dead initiated by Jesus' death and resurrection "on the third day" (16:21; 17:23; 20:19) indicates for the reader how Jesus has the power to rebuild God's temple within three days.

The Jewish leaders' opposition to Jesus does not cease with his death. When first the scribes and Pharisees (12:38–40) and later the Pharisees and Sadducees (16:1–4) sought a "sign" from Jesus, he cryptically referred to his resurrection by pointing them to the sign of Jonah the prophet: "Just as Jonah was in the belly of the whale three days and three nights (Jon 1:17), so will the Son of Man be in the heart of the earth three days and three nights" (12:40; see also 16:4). Recalling this "sign" indicating Jesus' resurrection "after three days" (27:63), the chief priests and the Pharisees urge Pilate to secure the tomb of Jesus in an effort to prevent a deceptive "resurrection" through theft of his corpse by the disciples (27:62–66). Even after their attempt to block Jesus' resurrection proves futile (28:2–4), the Jewish leaders concoct a false report that the disciples stole the body of Jesus, a fraudulent story that has circulated among the Jews to the time of the reader (28:11–15).[7]

Predictions of Passion, Death, and Resurrection

Jesus' announcements of his passion, death, and resurrection to his disciples alert the reader to what will happen to Jesus in the last chapters of the Matthean narrative:

> From that time on Jesus began to show his disciples that he must go to Jerusalem and suffer greatly from the elders, the chief priests, and the scribes, and be killed and on the third day be raised. (16:21)
>
> As they were gathering in Galilee, Jesus said to them, "The Son of Man is to be delivered into the hands of men, and they will kill him, and on the third day he will be raised." And they were deeply saddened. (17:22–23)
>
> As Jesus was going up to Jerusalem, he took the twelve disciples aside by themselves, and on the way said to them, "Behold, we are going up to Jerusalem, and the Son of Man will be delivered to the chief priests and scribes, and they will condemn him to death, and deliver him to the Gentiles to be mocked and scourged and crucified, and on the third day he will be raised." (20:17–19)

After Jesus has entered Jerusalem (21:1–11) and completed "all the words" of his previous teachings (26:1), with complete and majestic control he himself sets in motion the fulfillment of his previous passion predictions, as he announces to his disciples, "You know that after two days will be the Passover, and the Son of Man will be delivered to be crucified" (26:2). This climactic prediction serves as the cue for the Jewish leaders to play their role in putting Jesus to death. After Jesus has authoritatively reiterated his previous predictions that as "Son of Man" (17:22; 20:18) he will be "delivered" (17:22; 20:18–19) to be "crucified" (20:19), "then" and only then do "the chief priests and elders of the people" assemble in the palace of the high priest to conspire to kill him (26:3–4). These powerful predictions not only assure the reader of Jesus' superiority over the Jewish leaders—he knows beforehand exactly what they will do to him—but also enable the reader to interpret what they do to him as their unwitting fulfillment of the divine necessity that he "must" be killed and be raised (16:21).

As the narrative progresses the Jewish authorities play their roles as Jesus has predicted: When Judas betrays Jesus, he is accompanied by a large crowd from "the chief priests and elders of the people" (26:47). After Jesus is arrested, he is led away to the high priest, where "the scribes and the elders" were assembled (26:57), and where "the chief priests" and the entire Sanhedrin kept seeking false testimony against him to put him to death (26:59). The next morning all "the chief priests and the elders of the people" take counsel against Jesus to put him to death (27:1). When they then "delivered" him to Pilate the governor (27:2), they begin to fulfill Jesus' prediction that they would "deliver" him to the Gentiles to be "mocked and scourged and crucified" (20:19), which the soldiers of Pilate complete when they "mock" him, strike him on the head, and lead him off to "crucify" him (26:29–31). At his trial before Pilate "the chief priests and the elders" not only accuse him (27:12) but persuade the crowds to ask for the release of the criminal Barabbas and to destroy Jesus (27:20). All three groups mentioned in the passion predictions—"the chief priests with the scribes and elders"—mock Jesus dying on the cross (27:41). Finally, Jesus' repeated assertion that "on the third day he will be raised" (16:21; 17:23; 20:19) prepares not only for the attempt by "the chief priests" and the Pharisees to prevent the predicted resurrection of Jesus (27:62–64), and for the false report spread by "the chief priests with the elders" after Jesus has been raised (28:11–15), but also for the angel's declaration to the women at the tomb that he has been raised "just as he said" (28:6–7).

Resurrection from the Dead

As part of his divinely endowed authority to bring about the kingdom of God by healing and exorcising (12:28), Jesus possesses the power to raise people from the dead, as dramatically demonstrated when he raises an official's daughter back to life (9:18–26). When Jesus sends out his disciples to extend his proclamation of the arrival of the kingdom of heaven (10:7) with the authority to heal and exorcise, he includes the power to "raise the dead" (10:8). That "the dead are raised" is then listed together with healings and preaching as "the deeds of the Christ" (11:2–5). These raisings from the dead as restorations to mortal human life are surpassed by Jesus' own eschatological resurrection from the dead to a new, transcendent, and immortal life, which anticipates the expected general resurrection of the dead preliminary to God's final judgment.

That Jesus will be buried in the heart of the earth for "three days and three nights" (12:40) and will be raised "on the third day" (16:21; 17:23; 20:19) or "after three days" (26:63) underlines the definitiveness of his death and thus points to the eschatological nature of his resurrection as a resurrection to an entirely new existence rather than as a resuscitation to mortal human life. The presupposition of a general resurrection oriented to the last judgment is indicated by Jesus' shocking statement to the scribes and Pharisees that "at the judgment" both the pagan men of Nineveh and the gentile queen of the south "will arise with this generation and condemn it" (12:41–42). The raising from their tombs of the bodies of many saints who had fallen asleep that takes place as a result of Jesus' death and resurrection (27:50–53) previews this expected general resurrection of the dead for the final judgment.

But resurrection from the dead also signifies God's vindication of those who suffer an unjust death while remaining innocent and obedient to God. That Herod thinks Jesus is John the Baptist "raised from the dead" (14:2) not only implies God's vindication of Herod's murder of John as a God-sent prophet (14:5) but also prepares the reader for Jesus' resurrection as his vindication for suffering the same destiny of an unjust death (17:9–13). Jesus' own resurrection from the dead (28:6–7) vindicates his pronouncement that God raises the dead to an entirely new, angel-like existence in contradiction to the Sadducees' ridiculing denial and inadequate conception of resurrection (22:23–33). The resurrection of the many "saints" initiated by the death and resurrection of Jesus (27:50–53) also points to the vindication of all the righteous blood of the many "prophets, wise men and scribes" continually murdered by Jesus' Jewish opponents and their ancestors (23:29–36).

Finally, the appearance of the risen Jesus, endowed by God with "all power in heaven and on earth" (28:18), to his disciples in Galilee vindicates his unjust death by the Jewish authorities who mocked him as their messianic King and Son of God unable to save himself from death (27:41–43, 54). The promise of the risen Jesus that "I am with you all days until the end of the age" (28:20) assures the reader of Jesus' abiding salvific presence, while awaiting his predicted coming at the end of time to execute the final judgment and consummation of the kingdom of heaven that his resurrection from the dead anticipates (24:29–31; 25:31–46; 26:64).

NOTES

1. We are following the definition of the implied reader proposed by B. C. Lategan, "Reference: Reception, Redescription and Reality," in *Text and Reality: Aspects of Reference in Biblical Texts,* ed. B. C. Lategan and W. S. Vorster (Atlanta: Scholars, 1985) 70:

> The implied reader represents the response the author is aiming at or assuming on the part of his audience. In this sense it functions as a heuristic device to uncover the meaning of the text. It is a theoretical construct to gauge the intended effect of the text. The implied reader is on the receiving end of all the various indicators of the text. He experiences

> the full impact of all the strategies employed by the author, integrates the various elements, and projects the ideal response to the text, that is, a response congruent with the designs of the author as expressed in the text.

2. K. A. Plank (*Paul and the Irony of Affliction* [Atlanta: Scholars, 1987] 9) describes the response of the implied reader in terms of the "rhetorical effect" the text produces: "The *rhetorical effect* refers to the particular changes and affects which the author would incite in the readers as they progress through the text. Taken broadly, the rhetorical effect is the possible actualization of the text which the author intends to promote in the reader. In this sense, the rhetorical effect coincides with the commitments summoned in the serious reception of the discourse."

3. For more discussion of reader-response criticism, see T. J. Keegan, *Interpreting the Bible: A Popular Introduction to Biblical Hermeneutics* (New York/ Mahwah, N.J.: Paulist, 1985) 73–108; R. M. Fowler, "Who Is 'the Reader' in Reader Response Criticism?" *Reader Response Approaches to Biblical and Secular Texts*, Semeia 31, ed. R. Detweiler (Decatur: Scholars, 1985) 5–23; J. L. Resseguie, "Reader-Response Criticism and the Synoptic Gospels," *JAAR* 52 (1984) 307–24; J. L. Staley, *The Print's First Kiss: A Rhetorical Investigation of the Implied Reader in the Fourth Gospel,* SBLDS 82 (Atlanta: Scholars, 1988) 21–49; R. W. Funk, *The Poetics of Biblical Narrative* (Sonoma: Polebridge, 1988) 34–38. W. S. Vorster, "The Reader in the Text: Narrative Material," *Reader Perspectives on the New Testament*, Semeia 48, ed. E. V. McKnight (Atlanta: Scholars, 1989) 21–39.

4. J. P Heil, "Reader-Response and the Irony of Jesus before the Sanhedrin in Luke 22:66–71," *CBQ* 51 (1989) 272.

5. J. P. Heil, "Significant Aspects of the Healing Miracles in Matthew," *CBQ* 41 (1979) 274–87.

6. J. P. Meier, "John the Baptist in Matthew's Gospel," *JBL* 99 (1980) 383–405.

7. J. D. Kingsbury, "The Developing Conflict between Jesus and the Jewish Leaders in Matthew's Gospel: A Literary-Critical Study," *CBQ* 49 (1987) 57–73.

CHAPTER 2

Jesus Prepares for and Accepts His Death (Matt 26:1–56)

Jesus Anticipates His Death by Jewish Leaders (Matt 26:1–16)

Jewish Leaders Plot the Arrest and Death of Jesus (a[1] 26:1–5)

> [1]When Jesus finished all these words, he said to his disciples, [2]"You know that after two days will be the Passover, and the Son of Man will be delivered to be crucified." [3]Then the chief priests and the elders of the people assembled in the palace of the high priest, who was called Caiaphas, [4]and they consulted together to arrest Jesus by deceit and kill him. [5]But they said, "Not during the feast, lest there be a tumult among the people."

The death of Jesus during Passover (26:1–2). With its addition of the term *all* to the formula that concluded each of Jesus' previous teaching discourses—the sermon on the mount (5–7), the missionary discourse (10), the parable discourse (13), and the community discourse (18), the announcement that Jesus has "finished *all* these words" brings to a solemn conclusion not only the fifth and final discourse, the eschatological discourse (24–25), but "all" of the words of Jesus' previous teaching:

> When Jesus finished these words (7:28)
> When Jesus finished instructing his twelve disciples (11:1)
> When Jesus finished these parables (13:53)
> When Jesus finished these words (19:1)
> When Jesus finished *all* these words (26:1)

Now that Jesus has completed all of his teaching discourses, he prepares his disciples and the reader for the events of his passion, death, and resurrection with words reminiscent of Moses preparing the Israelites to enter the Promised Land after his death (LXX Deut 31:1–2; 32:44–46).[1] Having just instructed his disciples in the eschatological discourse to be always ready for his glorious coming as the messianic

"Son of Man" at the end of the age, Jesus now reminds them of the suffering and death he must endure as "Son of Man" preliminary to that final coming.[2]

The introduction of Jesus' prediction that as the Son of Man he "will be delivered to be crucified" with the notice that "after two days will be the Passover" not only alerts the reader to the imminent fulfillment of the passion he has repeatedly foretold to his disciples (16:21; 17:12, 22–23; 20:17–19) but also places the death of Jesus into the interpretive framework of the great Jewish feast of Passover. At the annual Passover festival the many pilgrims who filled Jerusalem commemorated not only their participation in the past saving deeds of God on behalf of the Israelites of old, especially their liberation from slavery in Egypt (Exodus 12), but also their anticipation of participating in God's future and final salvation. That Jesus will be put to death in accord with God's salvific design during the Passover leads the reader to realize that the sacrificial death of Jesus as the Son of Man who came to give his life as a "ransom" or "liberation" (*lytron*) for many (20:28) represents that final salvation which the Passover anticipates.

The death of Jesus apart from Passover? (26:3–5). As soon as Jesus has authoritatively announced the imminence of his passion and death, "then" (*tote*), and only then, do the "chief priests and elders of the people" gather in the palace of the high priest Caiaphas to play their role in bringing it about (26:3). But their decision "to arrest Jesus by deceit and kill him" (26:4) has already been encompassed by the superior authority and foreknowledge of Jesus. That they plan to "arrest him by deceit" simply develops Jesus' prediction that he "will be delivered or handed over" (*paradidotai*) with its connotation of "betrayal."[3] And that they will "kill" him has already been more precisely predicted by Jesus as "to be crucified." The reader is thus assured of Jesus' supremacy over the Jewish leaders as they unwittingly fulfill the divine necessity previously pronounced by Jesus—that he "must" suffer and die at their hands (16:21; 17:22–23; 20:18).

Suspense emerges for the reader as the Jewish authorities proclaim, "Not during the feast, lest there be a tumult among the people" (26:5). This directly contradicts Jesus' pronouncement that he would be delivered to be crucified during the Passover feast (26:2). The Jewish leaders must resort to "deceit" or "treachery" (*dolos*) to arrest and kill Jesus apart from the people gathered for the Passover because of his popularity among the crowds in Jerusalem who regard him as a prophet (21:11, 46). That "the chief priests and elders of *the people*" (*tou laou*, 26:3) want to prevent "a tumult of *the people*" (*tō laō*, 26:5) subtly underlines the conflict that has been developing between Jesus and the Jewish authorities with regard to authentic leadership of the people. By his activities in the Jerusalem temple, especially his masterful teaching, Jesus clearly demonstrated his superior ability to lead the people in contrast to the inadequate leadership of the various groups of Jewish authorities, whom he bested and subdued one after the other (21–23). But what will now come of the Jewish leaders' deceitful attempt to dissociate the divinely willed, salvific death of Jesus from "the people" celebrating God's past and future salvation in the Passover feast?

The Death of Jesus Is Anticipated During a Meal (b^1 26:6–13)

> [6]When Jesus was in Bethany in the house of Simon the leper, [7]a woman possessing an alabaster flask of costly perfumed ointment approached him and poured it on his head while he was reclining at table. [8]Seeing this, the disciples were indignant, saying, "Why this waste? [9]It could have been sold for much and given to the poor." [10]Aware of this, Jesus said to them, "Why do you make trouble for the woman? She has performed a good work toward me. [11]The poor you always have with you, but you will not always have me. [12]In pouring this perfumed ointment upon my body, she did it to prepare me for burial. [13]Amen I say to you, wherever this gospel is proclaimed in the whole world, what she has done will be told in memory of her."

A woman anoints Jesus with costly ointment (26:6–7). The ominous assembly of the chief priests and elders of the people "in the palace of the high priest" to arrest and kill Jesus by deceit (26:3–4) contrasts with the gathering of Jesus for table fellowship with his disciples "in Bethany in the house of Simon the leper" (26:6). Rather than reside in Jerusalem during his controversial teaching in the temple, Jesus had spent the night with his own group of followers in Bethany (21:17). That Jesus is again "in Bethany" continues to indicate his opposition to the corrupted Jerusalem temple and the Jewish leaders he has condemned for turning it into "a den of thieves" rather than a place of authentic worship as God's "house of prayer" (21:13). In Galilee the Pharisees had objected to Jesus' eating and thus establishing the sacred bond of meal fellowship with such social outcasts as public sinners and toll collectors (9:10–13). That Jesus is now in the house of "Simon the leper" means he is again associating with social outcasts and those who "need a physician" (9:12), to the disapproval of the Jewish leadership, who banned anyone with diseases such as leprosy from communal worship (8:1–4; 21:14–16).[4]

Continuing the antithesis to the high priest named Caiaphas, an unnamed woman with an alabaster flask of very expensive perfumed ointment approaches Jesus. She boldly performs a striking gesture of hospitality often part of communal meals (Pss 23:5; 133:2; 141:5; Luke 7:46), as she anoints the reclining Jesus by pouring the precious and fragrant oil over his head (26:7).

The disciples protest with concern for the poor (26:8–9). But conflict arises as the disciples angrily object to the woman's act of hospitality. Interpreting her deed as a "waste" of expensive ointment, they question what she has done (26:8) and point out that the valuable ointment could have been sold for a large sum and the proceeds given as alms to support the poor.[5] That the disciples value giving alms to the poor as more important than this hospitable anointing of Jesus (26:9) causes the reader to wonder whether they have appreciated Jesus' pronouncement of the imminence and significance of his death during the Passover (26:2).

Jesus explains that she has prepared him for burial (26:10–13). With the question "Why do you make trouble for the woman?" Jesus counters his disciples' anger and begins his defense of the woman. Rather than an extravagant waste of money and a missed opportunity for exercising almsgiving as an important duty of Jewish piety, Jesus designates the woman's gesture as a "good work" (*ergon kalon*), that is, an act of charity also valued by Jewish piety, which she has performed not toward the poor but "toward me," Jesus himself (26:10). Her "good work" toward Jesus thus stands in sharp contrast to the Jewish leaders' "deceit" (*dolos*) in their attempt to arrest and kill him (26:3–4).

By pointing to his future absence, Jesus emphasizes the uniqueness of his situation of need. He reminds his disciples that since they will always have the poor with them (Deut 15:11), they may and should fulfill their obligation of almsgiving whenever they wish. But the important point for them to realize is that they will not always have Jesus with them (9:14–15). That is what makes this occasion of table fellowship uniquely urgent and the woman's act of loving devotion so extremely valuable. As a practice of Jewish piety the merit of her "good work," then, surpasses that of almsgiving since it demonstrates a personal commitment of love for the specific person of Jesus at a time of urgent need rather than an impersonal giving to the general group of the poor always in need (26:11).[6]

Jesus then divulges that by pouring the perfumed ointment upon his body the woman has actually performed a prophetic gesture "to prepare me for burial" (26:12). By lavishly expending the precious oil she had in her possession to demonstrate her loving devotion to Jesus, this anonymous woman steps forward as a sterling model of true discipleship. With her notable esteem for the value of Jesus' upcoming death, she stands in distinct divergence to the male disciples, who fail to appreciate the imminence and significance of the death he has foretold to them (26:2).

With the solemn introductory words "Amen I say to you," Jesus further extols the woman's loving acknowledgment of his approaching death by announcing that in the future worldwide proclamation of the gospel her act of love will be told as part of the gospel message in "memory" of her (26:13). This authoritative pronouncement brings the contrast with the previous scene to an ironic climax. Whereas the chief priests and elders of the people are deceitfully trying to avoid involving "the people" in the death of Jesus during their celebration of the Passover feast (26:3–5), Jesus announces that his death will have an impact not only for "the people" of Israel but for all peoples of the "whole world." The "memorial" (*mnēmosynon*) of what this woman has done in reverently anticipating the precious value of his death will thus continue and far surpass the "memorial" of the Jewish Passover festival, which commemorates the saving event of the exodus as well as all of God's other saving deeds, past, present, and future.[7] The global proclamation of the gospel will memorialize forever and everywhere this nameless woman's anticipation of the death of Jesus as God's definitive saving deed for all peoples.

Through sharp contrast with the previous scene (26:1–5), then, the woman's "good work" in anointing Jesus for burial (26:6–13) assures the reader that, although the chief priests and elders of the people are trying by "deceit" to arrest Jesus and have him quietly put to death in separation from "the people" and their Passover festival, the esteemed and enduring value of Jesus' death as the saving event for all peoples, now anticipated in the celebration of table fellowship with his followers, will be proclaimed forever and everywhere "in the whole world" (26:13). Indeed, the reader is reminded that the followers of Jesus have the duty not only to proclaim the gospel "throughout the whole world as a witness to all peoples" before the end of the world (24:14) but to include in that global evangelization the "memory" of this extraordinary woman's loving acknowledgment of the precious death of Jesus as a crucial part of the gospel message (26:13).

A Disciple Plans to Betray Jesus to Death (a² 26:14–16)

> [14]Then one of the Twelve, who was called Judas Iscariot, went to the chief priests [15]and said, "What are you willing to give me if I betray him to you?" They paid him thirty pieces of silver. [16]And from that time on he was seeking an opportune time to betray him.

The chief priests pay Judas to betray Jesus (26:14–15). As the final scene in this first a-b-a intercalation,[8] Judas's offer to betray Jesus (26: 14–16) not only contrasts with the middle *b* scene of the sandwich (26:6–13) but also develops the thematic of the opening *a* scene (26:1–5).

In strong contrast to the previous meal fellowship established at Bethany between Jesus and his disciples and other followers, Judas Iscariot, although one of Jesus' specially chosen "Twelve" disciples (10:1–4), separates himself from close union with Jesus and joins the opposition of the Jewish leaders, as he goes "to the chief priests" (26:14). That Judas is explicitly "named" (*legomenos*) links him with the explicitly "named" (*legomenou*) high priest Caiaphas (26:3), and thus underlines his separation from the anonymous disciples and woman who remain in fellowship with Jesus.[9]

The contrast continues as Judas asks the chief priests, "What are you willing to give me if I betray him to you?" (26:15). Whereas the disciples were altruistically concerned with what could be "given" (*dothēnai*) to the poor (26:9), while Jesus pointed out the importance of the charitable deed the woman had performed "toward me" (*eis eme*, 26:10), Judas is selfishly concerned with what the chief priests will "give" (*dounai*) to "me" (*moi*). That they "paid him thirty pieces of silver" (26:15), the same contemptuous amount paid as wages to the rejected prophet/shepherd in Zech 11:12, the paltry sum paid for a gored slave (Exod 21:32),[10] stands in pathetic contrast to the woman's very expensive ointment (26:7–9). Whereas the woman expended her valuable ointment to anoint Jesus for burial, Judas greedily accepts from the chief priests a mere thirty pieces of silver to betray his master to death.

But Judas's offer to "betray him to you" (26:15) also advances the "deceit" against Jesus introduced in the opening scene (26:1–5) of this first intercalation. In accepting Judas's offer, the chief priests have now apparently found a way to arrest and kill Jesus by deceit to avoid a disturbance of the people during the Passover feast. The deceit will take the form of furtive betrayal by Judas, "one of the Twelve," a member of the group of disciples closest to Jesus.

From the time that Jesus chose the Twelve the reader has known that

Judas would be the one "who betrayed him" (10:4). That Judas now offers to "betray" (*paradōsō*) him to the "chief priests" confirms Jesus' authoritative pronouncement in the opening scene: "the Son of Man will be delivered [*paradidotai*] to be crucified" (26:2). The necessity for Jesus to be "delivered" or "betrayed" (*paradidosthai*, 17:22; *paradothēsetai*, 20:18) to the "chief priests" (16:21; 20:18) and other Jewish authorities in order to be put to death in accord with God's salvific plan, as repeatedly predicted by Jesus, is now being fulfilled. The reader can thus be assured that although it is a tragic betrayal, Judas's wicked scheme against Jesus is embraced within God's program of salvation.

Judas seeks an opportune time to betray Jesus (26:16). As soon as he became a bribed agent of the chief priests, Judas "was seeking an opportune time to betray him" (26:16). The "opportune time" (*eukairian*, literally, "good time") for Judas would be apart from the Passover feast, so as to avoid a tumult among the people (26:5). But the opportune time for Judas as the unwitting agent of God's salvific plan pronounced by Jesus would be during the Passover (26:2), when the people are appropriately commemorating God's great acts of salvation now to be climaxed by the sacrificial death of Jesus as a "ransom for many" (20:28). The suspense for the reader now centers on when this opportune time will arise.

Jesus Prepares the Disciples for His Death (Matt 26:17–29)

Jesus Directs His Disciples to Prepare the Passover Meal (b^2 26:17–19)

> 17On the first day of the feast of Unleavened Bread the disciples approached Jesus and said, "Where do you want us to prepare for you to eat the Passover?" 18He said, "Go into the city to a certain man and tell him, 'The Teacher says, "My appointed time is near; in your house I will celebrate the Passover with my disciples."'" 19Then the disciples did as Jesus had instructed them and prepared the Passover.

The disciples ask where Jesus wants to eat the Passover (26:17). Forming a b-a-b intercalation with the two previous scenes, the disciples' preparation for the Passover meal (26:17–19) not only contrasts with Judas's offer to betray Jesus to death (26:14–16) but also develops the theme of close union with Jesus introduced by his anointing for death during a meal (26:6–13).

With the notice that it is already "the first day of the feast of Unleavened Bread" (26:17)—that is, the beginning of the weeklong celebration that coincided with the Passover and commemorated the hasty exit of Israel from Egypt, when they could take only unleavened bread (Exodus 12), the reader experiences the mounting suspense about the timing of the betrayal. The Passover is already beginning, but Judas had wanted to betray Jesus to the chief priests and elders of the people at "an opportune time" (26:16), that is, at a time apart from the Passover festival and "the people" celebrating it (26:3–5).

In contrast to Judas, the disciple who after abandoning table fellowship with Jesus (26:6–13) and going to the chief priests, asks, "What are you willing [*thelete*] to give me [*moi*] if I betray him to you?" (26:15), the disciples who remain with Jesus ask him, "Where do you want [*theleis*] us to prepare for you [*soi*] to eat the Passover?" (26:17). Whereas Judas violates his discipleship by submitting himself to the chief priests with his selfish concern for what they are "willing" to give "me," the rest of the disciples remain in submission to their master with their concern for where Jesus "wants" them to prepare for "you" to eat the Passover. Against the foil of the perfidious plot of a defected disciple, then, the reader is assured that there are still obedient disciples who want to play their part in enabling the sacrificial death of their master—as the definitive act of God's salvation—to take place during the Passover as Jesus predicted (26:2).

As the Teacher, Jesus directs his disciples (26:18–19). But this scene of the disciples' preparation for Jesus' special Passover meal also advances the theme of their intimate union with Jesus begun by the first b scene, his anointing for death during the meal in Bethany (26:6–13). That Jesus now sends his disciples into Jerusalem to prepare his final Passover meal with authoritative instructions as their "teacher" indicates his strong intent to eat the Passover meal with "my disciples" (26:18) in view of his impending death, despite the deceitful attempt of the Jewish leaders to prevent that death from taking place during the Passover (26:3–5).[11] That Jesus has already been anointed for burial (26:12) lends added significance to this particular Passover meal, as it places his impending death in the context of the Passover commemoration of God's deeds of salvation on behalf of his people. The reader thus realizes that Jesus' authoritative foreknowledge of God's plan for his death eclipses his enemies' plot.

The "certain man" in Jerusalem to whom Jesus sends his disciples

(26:18) complements the nameless "woman" in Bethany. As the woman performed a prophetic gesture of hospitality that prepared for Jesus' burial, so the anonymous man now provides the hospitality of his home so that Jesus, the Teacher, can share the table fellowship of this special Passover meal with his disciples in view of his death.

In directing his disciples to prepare the Passover meal, Jesus empowers them to use his authority as "*the* Teacher" (*ho didaskalos*). They are to tell the "certain man" in Jerusalem: "The Teacher says, 'My appointed time is near; in your house I will celebrate the Passover with my disciples'" (26:18). While many have addressed and referred to Jesus as "teacher" throughout the narrative,[12] and Jesus has indirectly referred to himself as "teacher" (10:24–25; 23:8), this is the first and final time that Jesus directly refers to himself as teacher, indeed, as "*the* Teacher," the one who "teaches" the crowds with divine "authority" and "not as their scribes" (7:28–29). By identifying himself as *the* Teacher, Jesus not only brings to a demonstrative climax the previous references to him as teacher but confirms the divine authority of all his previous teachings.[13] This is also the first and only time that Jesus refers to his disciples as "*my* disciples" (*tōn mathētōn mou*, 26:18). This emphasizes the close teacher-disciple bond uniting Jesus with his followers, a bond Jesus strongly desires to deepen with "*my* disciples" through the table fellowship of this special Passover meal.

By underlining the imminence of his death during the Passover (26:2), now that he has been anointed for burial (26:12), the authoritative statement that Jesus as the Teacher empowers his disciples to announce, namely, that "my appointed time [*kairos*] is near" (26:18), overshadows Judas's attempt to find "an opportune time" (*eukairian*) to betray him (26:16), a time separate from the Passover feast (26:3–5). It is through Jesus' superior authority as the Teacher that his disciples are able to "prepare" (26:17, 19) for this special meal in anticipation of Jesus' salvific death. That the disciples obediently prepared the Passover exactly "as Jesus had instructed them" (26:19) underscores his authoritative direction of the events of God's plan of salvation and further assures the reader of the truth of all that Jesus, the Teacher, has taught and predicted, especially the events of his passion, death, and resurrection. Thus, in defiant antithesis to the insidious intrigue of Judas and the Jewish leaders to prevent Jesus' death during the Passover, the obedient disciples have prepared the Passover meal to seal their special teacher-disciple bond with Jesus, the authoritative Teacher, in anticipation of the salvific death for which he has already been anointed.

Jesus Predicts His Betrayal by Judas (a³ 26:20–25)

> 20When it became evening Jesus reclined at table with the Twelve.
> 21And while they were eating, he said, "Amen I say to you, one of you will
> betray me." 22Deeply saddened, they began to say to him one after
> another, "Surely it is not I, Lord?" 23In reply he said, "He who has dipped
> his hand in the dish with me is the one who will betray me. 24The Son of
> Man indeed goes as it is written about him, but woe to that man by whom
> the Son of Man is betrayed. It would be better for that man if he had never
> been born." 25In reply Judas, his betrayer, said, "Surely it is not I, Rabbi?"
> He said to him, "You have said it."

Jesus announces his betrayal by one of the Twelve (26:20–22). Forming an a-b-a sandwich with the two previous scenes, Jesus' prediction of his betrayal by one of his chosen Twelve (26:20–25) not only stands in tragic contrast to the preparation for the celebration of the teacher-disciple bond between Jesus and his Twelve disciples within the table fellowship of the Passover meal (26:17–19) but also advances the theme of Judas's offer to betray Jesus to those seeking his arrest and death (26:14–16).

Once it "became evening" on the first day of the feast of Unleavened Bread (26:17), Jesus "reclined at table" to share the fellowship of the Passover meal "with the Twelve" (26:20). That Jesus reclines "*with* the Twelve" (*meta tōn dōdeka*) not only fulfills his intention as the Teacher to deepen his teacher-disciple bond by celebrating the Passover "*with* my disciples" (*meta tōn mathētōn mou*) (26:18) but also reminds the reader that "one of the Twelve" (*heis tōn dōdeka*) is Judas (26:14). Precisely "while they were eating" and thus sharing the intimacy of fellowship, Jesus solemnly introduces a tragic incongruity to his close union with the Twelve disciples: "Amen I say to you, one of you will betray me" (26:21). "One" (*heis*) of you (the Twelve) "will betray [*paradōsei*] me" contrasts with the previous b scene by gravely violating the bond to be sealed at this Passover. It also advances the theme of the previous a scene by assuring the reader of Jesus' foreknowledge that "one [*heis*] of the Twelve" will "betray" (*paradōsō*, 26:15; *paradō*, 26:16) him.

In response to Jesus' shocking pronouncement of his betrayal, the disciples become "deeply saddened" (see also 17:23) as each of them, with genuine sorrow and obvious bewilderment, begins to object, "Surely it is not I, Lord?" (26:22). Their respectful address of Jesus as "Lord" (*kyrie*), aptly acknowledging his majestic authority,[14] continues to indicate the incongruous contrast with the previous scene. How can any of these faithful disciples, as those who properly prepared this Passover meal in obedience to their authoritative Teacher (26:17–19) and sovereign Lord, possibly be the one to betray him?

Jesus implicates Judas as his betrayer (26:23–25). By intensifying the betrayer's serious breach of intimate table fellowship with Jesus, Jesus' reply that "he who has dipped his hand in the dish with me [*met' emou*] is the one who will betray me" (26:23) continues the tragic contrast with the teacher-disciple bond the disciples established with Jesus in the previous scene. But Jesus' reply also develops his superior knowledge of the plan to betray him (26:14–16): He knows that one of the Twelve will betray him and precisely who the betrayer is. With a subtle allusion to Ps 41:9, "Even my bosom friend in whom I trusted, who ate of my bread, has lifted his heel against me" (see also Ps 55:12–14), Jesus' reply places him in the biblical tradition of the "suffering just one," the person who humbly remains loyal to God despite opposition and persecution, even from closest friends and companions, with the confidence that God will vindicate his faithfulness in ultimate triumph (Ps 41:10–12). The betrayer's violation of close union with Jesus, then, is encompassed by God's scriptural plan.

Illustrating his complete foreknowledge and determined acceptance of his role in God's future plan of salvation, Jesus continues his reply by proclaiming that as "the Son of Man" he indeed will go to his death "as it is written about him" (26:24)—that is, in accord with the "necessity" (16:21; 17:12, 22–23; 20:17–19) of God's scriptural plan. Although Jesus' betrayal by one of the Twelve is embraced by God's salvific will, the betrayer, held fully and personally responsible, is to be greatly pitied for breaking his intimate bond with Jesus and betraying him: "But woe to that man by whom the Son of Man is betrayed." Indeed, so unfortunate and accursed is the fate of the betrayer that it sadly would have been better if he had never even been born (26:24). The negative example of the one member of the Twelve stands in stark contrast to the positive model of the nameless woman who anointed Jesus:

> Wherever this gospel is proclaimed in the whole world, what she has done will be told in memory of her. (26:13)
>
> But woe to that man by whom the Son of Man is betrayed. It would be better for that man if he had never been born. (26:24)

Despite Jesus' severe condemnation, Judas, who had earlier asked the chief priests, "What are you willing to give me if I betray him to you?" (26:15), now coldly asks Jesus, "Surely it is not I, Rabbi?" (26:25). With its blatant insincerity and inadequate assessment of Jesus as "Rabbi" rather than "Lord," Judas's query differs notably from the genuine sorrow and submissive respect of the other disciples, who, with great sadness, asked, "Surely it is not I, Lord?" (26:22). Although Rabbi was a title of respect for a teacher (23:7–8), Lord is more appropriate for Jesus, the sovereign Teacher. The divergence of Judas's question underlines his separation from the rest of the disciples and their proper relationship to Jesus as their Lord. Jesus' indirect affirmation, "You have said it" (26:25), turns the question back on Judas and indicates that his own words have condemned him. Although the reader understands the tragedy that even a close disciple can break his bond with Jesus and betray him, the reader is assured of Jesus' resolute acceptance and superior foreknowledge of his betrayal in accord with God's plan.

Through the Passover Meal, Jesus and His Disciples Share in His Triumph Over Death (b³ 26:26–29)

> [26]While they were eating, Jesus took bread, blessed and broke it, and giving it to the disciples said, "Take and eat; this is my body." [27]Then taking a cup and giving thanks, he gave it to them, saying, "Drink from it, all of you, [28]for this is my blood of the covenant, which will be poured out for many for the forgiveness of sins. [29]I tell you, from now on I shall not drink from this fruit of the vine until that day when I drink it with you new in the kingdom of my Father."

Jesus designates the bread of the meal as his body (26:26). The sharing of Jesus and his Twelve disciples in his triumph over death through their special Passover meal (26:26–29) concludes a b-a-b intercalation with the two previous scenes. It contrasts with Jesus' prediction during the meal of his betrayal by one of the Twelve (26:20–25) and develops the theme of their close teacher-disciple relationship introduced by the preparation for the Passover meal (26:17–19).

While the disciples and Jesus are "eating" the special Passover meal the disciples have prepared through the authoritative command of Jesus, the Teacher (26:17–19), he performs the role of host or head of the meal by taking "bread," "blessing" or thanking God for it, "breaking" it for distribution, and "giving" it to his disciples (26:26). In the ritual of the Passover meal the father or head of the household pronounces the traditional symbolic interpretations upon the various elements of the meal, so that the participants can not only commemorate but actually share in and sacramentally relive the salvific experience of the original Passover meal, when God liberated his people from slavery in the exodus from Egypt and gave them the hope of future and final salvation. In his last Passover meal with his disciples, Jesus, as their Teacher, Lord, and host, transforms the meaning of this meal for them as he places a new symbolic interpretation upon the bread and wine.

After directing them to "take and eat" the bread he has blessed and broken for them, Jesus designates it as the symbolic and sacramental equivalent of his "body," that is, his very person: "This *is* my body." The bread thus becomes the very body or person of Jesus (*to sōma mou*, 26:26), which body (*tou sōmatos mou*, 26:12) has already been anointed for death and burial. By giving them the Passover bread, which is his body destined for death, to eat, Jesus enables his disciples to sacramentally share in his death as the salvific event that climaxes all the past saving deeds of God for his people. The Twelve's intimate teacher-disciple bond with Jesus (26:17–19) thus reaches its high point in this unique Passover meal as they eat the bread-body of Jesus, which unites them in special table fellowship with him on his way to death, against the foil of the prediction during that same meal (26:21) of Judas's tragic rupture of that bond (26:20–25).

This final meal climaxes the meal fellowship Jesus has shared with his disciples and others throughout the narrative (8:15; 9:9–17; 14:13–21; 15:32–39; 26:6–13). The ritual gestures of taking-blessing-breaking-giving that Jesus performs in offering the bread that is his body recall the corresponding gestures he used in both of the previous miraculous meals with the crowds:

> *Taking* the five *loaves* and the two fish, he looked up to heaven and *blessed* them, and *breaking* the loaves, he *gave* them to the disciples, and the disciples [gave them] to the crowds. (14:19)
>
> He *took* the seven *loaves* and the fish, *gave thanks, broke* the loaves, and *gave* them to the disciples, and the disciples [gave them] to the crowds. (15:36)
>
> Jesus *took bread, blessed* and *broke* it, and *giving* it to the disciples said, "*Take* and eat; this is my body." (26:26)

In the miraculous meals the pattern Jesus established by his gestures of taking-blessing-breaking-giving the bread concluded with his disciples distributing the bread to the crowds. This pattern implies that when the disciples "take" the Passover bread-body that Jesus "gives" them, they are not only to feed themselves but, as intermediaries for Jesus, to again distribute it to the people in future celebrations of this new Passover meal. The very nature of the traditional Passover meal as a repeatedly celebrated commemoration indicates that the disciples are also to celebrate again this new Passover meal of Jesus. In giving them the Passover bread that is his very person destined for death, Jesus has done two things: He has left his disciples a new way to be united with him after he has died, and he has enabled them to feed, satisfy, and unify other people with him and his saving death.

Jesus designates the wine as his blood (26:27–29). Continuing his special Passover meal, Jesus "takes" a "cup" of wine, "gives thanks" to God for it, and "gives" it to his disciples, with the command, "Drink from it, all of you" (26:27). That "all" (*pantes*) are to "drink" (*piete*) from the "cup" (*potērion*) Jesus gives them fulfills for all of the disciples on the literal level the previous promise Jesus made to James and John that they would "drink [*piesthe*] the cup [*potērion*]" that he "drinks," as a metaphor for sharing in his suffering and death before they enter into "glory" with him (20:20–23). The literal "drinking" from "the cup" that Jesus gives "all" the disciples, then, indicates their sacramental participation in the suffering and death of Jesus through this new Passover meal and thus prepares them for their own future sufferings and deaths (10:16–25; 24:9–13).

As he had reinterpreted the Passover bread as his own body destined for death, so now Jesus reinterprets the cup of wine as the symbolic and sacramental equivalent of his own "blood" about to be shed in his death: "This *is* my blood of the covenant, which will be poured out for many for the forgiveness of sins" (26:28). By designating the cup of wine as "my blood of the covenant," Jesus relates the blood to be shed by his death to the sacrificial "blood of the covenant" that Moses threw against the altar, representative of God, and upon the people (Exod 24:3–8) with the words "Behold the blood of the covenant which the Lord has made with you in accordance with all these words" (Exod 24:8). The ceremony establishing the covenant concluded with a meal that united the people of Israel in the covenantal relationship with God (Exod 24:9–11).

In the biblical tradition "covenant" referred to the fundamental relationship uniting God to Israel as his specially chosen people, the pledge of mutual fidelity and loyalty according to which God would be their saving God and they would be his people.[15] But the people of Israel repeatedly failed to uphold their role in God's covenant with them. Consequently God, through prophecies such as those pronounced by Jeremiah, promised to establish a new, permanent, and definitive covenant with his people. This new covenant would be profoundly internal to the people, "written upon their hearts," and characterized by a universal knowledge of God and the forgiveness of sins (Jer 31:31–34; 32:37–41). By referring to his blood as "my blood of the covenant," Jesus indicates that the blood of his death will effect the fulfillment of the "covenant," the new and definitive covenant according to which God unites himself permanently and profoundly with his people in a salvific and liberating relationship.[16] Jesus thus further transforms the Passover meal into a covenant meal, whereby those who drink the wine designated as his blood of *the* covenant are sacramentally and profoundly united into this new and final covenantal relationship that God establishes with his people through the salvific death of Jesus.

That Jesus' blood, which effects *the* covenant with God, "will be poured out for many for the forgiveness of sins" emphasizes the nature of Jesus' death as a covenantal sacrifice for the atonement of sins. As the blood of sacrificed animals was "poured out" by priests on the altar as a sin offering to atone for the sins of the people (Lev 4:7, 18, 25, 30, 34), so the blood that will be "shed" or "poured out" by the death of Jesus represents a sacrifice for the atonement of sins "for," that is, "on behalf of" (*peri*), "many" people. The forgiveness of sins brought about by the sacrificial death of Jesus is part of the new and definitive covenant God establishes with his people (Jer 31:34). That the atoning blood of Jesus will be poured out on behalf of "many" (*pollōn*), a common Semitic expression for "all" people,[17] indicates the universal nature of the covenant, which brings forgiveness and salvation to "all." This corresponds to and develops Jesus' previous pronouncement that the selfless offering of his life will effect a salvific liberation for "many" = "all" people:

> For the Son of Man did not come to be served but to serve and to give his life as a ransom for many [*pollōn*]. (20:28)
>
> This is my blood of the covenant, which will be poured out for *many* [*pollōn*] for the forgiveness of sins. (26:28)

Thus the covenant established through the sacrificially atoning blood of Jesus is intended to include "all" people.

The contrast between the scenes in 26:20–25 and 26:26–29, each of which occurs while Jesus is sharing the table fellowship of the Passover meal with the Twelve—"while they were eating" (*esthiontōn autōn* in 26:21, 26)—becomes most evident in the reader's sequential experience of Jesus' solemn pronouncements in 26:21 and 26:29: That one of the Twelve who is eating with Jesus will betray him (26:21) and thus break his close teacher-disciple union means that Jesus will no longer drink wine, the festive drink produced from "this fruit of the vine" (26:29). This indicates not only that his death is very imminent but that it will prevent him from partaking of the joyous meal fellowship he has continually shared with his followers. But the death of Jesus through betrayal by one of the Twelve will not bring a definitive conclusion to the festivity of his table fellowship with his followers. On the contrary, the reader is assured that "on that day" of God's end-time fulfillment of his salvific activity, after Jesus' triumph over death through his resurrection, he will drink "new" festive wine and thus again be united in joyous meal fellowship with his followers in the "kingdom of my Father" (26:29).

Through Jesus' contrasting predictions (26:21, 29) the reader realizes that the death of Jesus will not only take place within the salvific context of the Passover, despite his betrayer's assistance (26:14–16) to the Jewish leaders' attempt to prevent this (26:3–5), but that it will have a future and definitive salvific effect beyond this particular Passover feast. The symbolic significance Jesus places upon his last Passover meal with the Twelve as an anticipatory sharing in his salvific death assures the reader that the death of Jesus will have a salvific effect not only for "the people" of Israel but for all peoples, despite and in ironic contrast to the betrayer's conspiracy with the Jewish authorities to prevent the death of Jesus from causing a "tumult among the people" (26:5). Jesus' designation of the wine of his unique Passover meal as the blood of the "covenant," that is, of the special relationship by which God united himself to Israel as his chosen people, indicates the salvific effect of Jesus' death for the people of Israel. And that the sacrificial "blood" of Jesus' death will be poured out for "many" points to the salvific effect of Jesus' death for all peoples.

Jesus Accepts Death through Prayer (Matt 26:30–56)

Jesus Predicts Abandonment/Denial by His Disciples (a[4] 26:30–35)

> [30]After singing a hymn, they went out to the Mount of Olives. [31]Then
> Jesus said to them, "All of you will fall away because of me this night, for it
> is written:
> 'I will strike the shepherd,
> and the sheep of the flock will be scattered' [Zech 13:7].
> [32]But after I have been raised up, I will go before you to Galilee." [33]In
> reply Peter said to him, "If all fall away because of you, I will never fall
> away." [34]Jesus said to him, "Amen I say to you, this very night before the
> cock crows you will deny me three times." [35]Peter said to him, "Even if I
> must die with you, I will not deny you." And all the disciples spoke
> likewise.

All the disciples will leave Jesus until he is raised (26:30–32). Forming an a-b-a sandwich with the two previous scenes, Jesus' prediction of his disciples' abandonment of him (26:30–35) not only contrasts with but also develops the theme of the previous scene, where Jesus united his disciples with his death through the Passover meal (26:26–29). It also develops and contrasts with Jesus' prediction of betrayal by a disciple (26:20–25).

The "singing of a hymn" by Jesus and his disciples marks the jubilant conclusion of the unique Passover meal,[18] which has united the disciples in a close bond of fellowship with Jesus by enabling them to sacramentally anticipate both his death and his future triumph. With their singing, the intimate relationship of the disciples with Jesus the Teacher reaches a high point as they conclude the meal. Jesus once again "went out" of Jerusalem with his disciples (21:17; 24:1) and returned not to the congenial setting of Bethany (21:17; 26:6–13) but to the Mount of Olives, where Jesus had prepared his disciples for their separation from him after his death and resurrection and before his coming in glory at the end of time (chaps. 24–25; 26:30).

In stunning contradiction to their intimate sharing in the previous b scene (26:26–29), Jesus foretells to his disciples that "all of you will fall away because of me this night." "All" of the disciples, who have just been closely united to Jesus on his way to death, as they were "all" invited to drink from the Passover cup of wine designated as the very blood of Jesus, will "fall away" and thus be separated from Jesus.

But Jesus' prediction of desertion by all of the disciples also develops the previous a scene (26:20–25) by complementing his earlier prediction of betrayal by "one" of the Twelve. Not only will "one" of the Twelve eating the Passover meal with Jesus violate his close bond with Jesus by betraying him (26:21–23) but "all" of the disciples who have just participated in that fellowship will also impede their intimate union with Jesus by "falling away" from him this very night.

That all the disciples will "fall away" or "stumble" over Jesus, literally "be scandalized" (*skandalisthēsesthe*) "because of me" (*en emoi*) (26:31), means that they will fail to heed Jesus' earlier appeal that "blessed is the one who does not stumble [*skandalisthē*] because of me [*en emoi*]" (11:6). They will be like the one in Jesus' parable who initially hears the word with joy, but, having no root in himself, "when tribulation or persecution because of the word arises, he immediately falls away [*skandalizetai*]" (13:21). They will be like those of Jesus' hometown and the Pharisees who "took offense" (*eskandalizonto*) at him (13:57; 15:12). And they will be like the many who "will fall away" (*skandalisthēsontai*) in infidelity before Jesus' final coming (24:10). The disciples' falling away or being scandalized thus demonstrates the shallowness of their faith in Jesus, which prevents them from following and remaining with him on his way to suffering and death.

Further developing the previous a scene (26:20–25), the disciples' desertion, like Judas's betrayal, accords with what "is written" explicitly in the scriptural plan of God. Not only will "one" of the Twelve violate his bond with Jesus by betraying him in accord with God's "written" (*gegraptai*) plan (26:24), but "all" of the disciples will impede their union with Jesus by falling away from him in accord with God's "written" (*gegraptai*) plan: "I will strike the shepherd, and the sheep of the flock will be scattered" (Zech 13:7 in 26:31).

The adaptation of the quotation from Zech 13:7 accentuates how the suffering and death of Jesus is the work of God himself. "I" (God himself) "will strike" with suffering and death "the shepherd" (Jesus), and consequently "the sheep of the flock" (the disciples) "will be scattered." The image of Jesus as "shepherd" was introduced in the infancy narrative (2:1–6), where the birth of Jesus in Bethlehem indicated that he was the expected messianic "ruler" who would "shepherd" God's people of Israel in fulfillment of the Scriptures (Mic 5:1; 2 Sam 5:2). As the true shepherd of Israel Jesus felt compassion for the crowds because they were troubled and abandoned, "like sheep without a shepherd" (Num 27:17; 1 Kgs 22:17 in 9:36). He then sent out his Twelve disciples with power to continue his healing ministry (10:1) toward these "lost sheep of the house of Israel" (10:6; see also 15:24). The deep "compassion" (9:36; 14:14; 15:32) of Jesus for the shepherdless crowds following him prompted him to demonstrate how he was the true shepherd-king of Israel (Ezek 34) by gathering them together and overabundantly feeding them (14:13–21; 15:32–38).[19] Now the close union that Jesus as "shepherd" has just established in his last Passover meal with his disciples will be broken as they "will be scattered" like "sheep" who disperse when the "shepherd" of the flock is killed (26:31).

But Jesus' prediction of abandonment and denial also further develops the theme in the previous b scene (26:26–29) of Jesus' close union with his disciples through their Passover table fellowship. The scattering of the disciples will only be temporary. After Jesus, the shepherd, has been raised from the dead, he will "go before" his disciples, like a "shepherd" leading the "sheep," and return "to Galilee" (26:32). In Galilee, the place where Jesus first called his disciples to follow him, the risen Jesus will renew the bond broken by the deserting disciples. Thus the reader realizes that Jesus will not only ultimately reestablish the intimacy of table fellowship with his disciples when he drinks of the new fruit of the vine in the kingdom of his Father (26:29) but, before that, after his resurrection from the dead, he will rejoin his disciples in Galilee, where they may follow him anew.[20]

Jesus' promise to go before them to Galilee does, however, contrast with the previous a scene. There Jesus had declared that it would have been better for Judas if he had never been born (26:24). But here the reader is assured that Jesus will reestablish his close union—now to be temporarily interrupted in accord with God's plan—with the rest of the disciples after he has been raised from the dead.

Peter will deny Jesus three times (26:33–35). In further contrast to the previous a scene (26:20–25), in which each of Twelve submissively said, "Surely it is not I, Lord" (26:22), after being deeply distressed by Jesus' prediction that one of them would betray him (26:21), Peter, the leader (10:2) and usual spokesman of the disciples (15:15; 16:16, 22; 17:4, 24; 18:21; 19:27), brashly contradicts Jesus' authoritative prediction that all the disciples will abandon him, even though it must happen in accord with Scripture (26:31): "If all fall away because of you, I will never fall away" (26:33). With his customary impetuosity (14:28) Peter now speaks only for himself. He insists that he will prove the exception.

Reinforcing and developing his shocking prediction of desertion by all his disciples, Jesus counters Peter's impulsive protest with a further, more intense and individualized prediction directed at Peter. With the solemn introductory formula, "Amen I say to you," emphasizing the certainty of what he will say, Jesus predicts that Peter, the first-called and leader of the disciples, will shamefully "deny" him. Jesus underlines how quickly and repeatedly Peter will deny him by stating that "this very night" before the cock has the chance to crow as a signal of dawn, Peter will "three times," that is, definitively, deny him (26:34).

In further contradiction to the previous b scene (26:26–29), in which the disciples have just anticipated the suffering and death of Jesus, Peter, in what functions as dramatic irony,[21] vehemently protests Jesus' prediction of his denial: "Even if I must die with you, I will not deny you" (26:35). Peter ironically does not seem to realize that a disciple "must" indeed "die with" Jesus. Unable to fulfill Jesus' demand that a disciple must "deny" (*aparnēsasthō*) oneself, "take up one's cross" and follow Jesus on the way to suffering and death (16:24; 10:38), Peter will fail miserably as a disciple by "denying" (*aparnēsē*, 26:34) Jesus rather than himself. Peter will not simply desert; he will sharpen his separation from Jesus by blatantly denying him. It is precisely because Peter has not grasped the necessity of suffering and "dying with" Jesus (16:22–23) that he will deny him. The reader sees in this the paradox that the necessity for a disciple to die with Jesus does not preclude denial of him—both dying with Jesus and denying him, as illustrated in Peter, are embraced by God's plan as predicted by Jesus.

Although Peter insistently and presumptuously maintains that he will be the one exception to desertion of Jesus, "all the disciples spoke likewise" (26:35), similarly protesting their abandonment of Jesus. And so "all" of the disciples, despite having anticipated the suffering and death of Jesus by drinking his cup of wine-blood (26:27–28), fail to understand that they cannot avoid abandoning Jesus because all of them will be scattered in accord with the written plan of God (26:31). But the hope remains sure that after Jesus' resurrection the disciples will rejoin him (26:32).

While Still with His Disciples Jesus Accepts Death through Prayer (b^4 26:36–46)

> 36Then Jesus came with them to a place called Gethsemane, and he
> said to the disciples, "Sit here while I go over there and pray." 37He took
> along Peter and the two sons of Zebedee, and began to be saddened and
> distressed. 38Then he said to them, "I am very sorrowful, even to death.
> Remain here and watch with me."
>
> 39And going forward a little, he fell prostrate in prayer, saying, "My
> Father, if it is possible, let this cup pass from me; but not as I will but as
> you will!"
>
> 40He returned to the disciples and found them sleeping, and said to
> Peter, "So you could not watch with me for one hour? 41Watch and pray,
> so that you may not enter the test. The spirit is willing but the flesh is
> weak."
>
> 42Withdrawing a second time, he prayed again, saying, "My Father, if it
> is not possible that this cup pass without my drinking it, your will be
> done!"
>
> 43Returning again he found them asleep, for their eyes were heavy.
> 44He left them and withdrew again and prayed a third time, saying the
> same thing again. 45Then he returned to the disciples and said to them,
> "Are you still sleeping and taking your rest? Behold, the hour has arrived
> and the Son of Man is betrayed into the hands of sinners. 46Get up, let us
> go! Behold, my betrayer has arrived!"

While Jesus prays, the disciples are to keep watch (26:36–38). Related to the two previous scenes in a b-a-b intercalation, Jesus' prayer in Gethsemane with his disciples (26:36–46) not only contrasts with but also develops the theme of separation from Jesus in the previous scene of Jesus' prediction of his disciples' abandonment and denial (26:30–35). It also develops and contrasts with the theme of close union with Jesus in the scene of Jesus' Passover table fellowship with his disciples (26: 26–29).

Against the foil of his prediction of the disciples' separation from him in the previous a scene (26:30–35), Jesus now continues the close union he established with them through the Passover meal in the previous b scenes (26:17–19, 26–29) as he comes "with them" (*met' autōn*; see also "with my disciples" [*meta tōn mathētōn mou*] in 26:18 and "with you" [*meth' hymōn*] in 26:29) to a place on the Mount of Olives known as Gethsemane (26:36). Although still with his disciples, Jesus begins to separate himself from them for the purpose of praying alone. He directs the disciples to "sit here while I go over there and pray" (26:36). Jesus had similarly prayed alone on a mountain (14:23) before he revealed to his disciples his divine power to walk on the sea and save them from the sea storm (14:22–33). Jesus' desire again to pray alone prepares the reader for another critical revelation of Jesus to his disciples.

Withdrawing from the larger group of disciples, Jesus takes with him the special smaller group composed of "Peter and the two sons of Zebedee [James and John]" (26:37). Jesus chose these three to accompany him as witnesses to the revelation of his heavenly glory in the scene of his transfiguration (17:1–8). Now that the time has arrived for Jesus' suffering and death preliminary to that heavenly glory, he appropriately takes these same three disciples to be close companions and witnesses of his sadness and distress over approaching death.

The expected critical event commences with a notable change in the emotional state of Jesus as he "began to be saddened and distressed" (26:37). With allusions to the biblical psalms of lament and in accord with his portrayal as the "suffering just one" (Pss 40:12–13; 42:9–11; 55:5–6; 116:3–4; Sir 51:6–12), he announces the extreme seriousness of the situation to the three disciples: "I am very sorrowful, even to death" (26:38; see Pss 42:5, 11; 43:5; Jon 4:9). Jesus reveals that his quite human trepidation at approaching death is now overwhelming him with a deep distress and sorrow commensurate with that death.

Jesus then directs Peter and the two sons of Zebedee to "remain here and watch with me" (26:38). His anxious appeal for these three to watch "with me" (*met' emou*) stands in suspenseful contrast to his prediction in the previous a scene that all the disciples would fall away "because of me" (*en emoi*) this night (26:31). Jesus directly challenges the discipleship not only of the "sons of Zebedee," who brazenly avowed that they could "drink the cup" of suffering that Jesus was going to drink (20:22), but also of Peter, the one who boldly protested to Jesus that even if all the disciples fall away "because of you" (*en soi*), he would not (26:33), and that he would die "with you" (*syn soi*) rather than deny Jesus (26:35).

Jesus' urgent plea for these three disciples to "watch" (*grēgoreite*, 26:38) recalls his earlier command for the disciples and for all others to "watch" (*grēgoreite*, 24:42; 25:13) in the period after his resurrection and before his final coming as Son of Man in glory (24:36–44). To "watch" means to be awake and alert, ready and prepared for the crucial "day" and "hour" introducing God's final and definitive salvation. The disciples' watching while Jesus prays thus makes them a paradigm for the reader's time of "watching" for the final and triumphant coming of Jesus after his death and resurrection.

Jesus prays in accord with God's will (26:39). "Going forward a little," Jesus separates himself from Peter and the two sons of Zebedee a short distance. Although Jesus goes forward to pray alone, his praying has significance for the disciples, who, though separated, are still in close proximity to Jesus. Indeed, the praying of Jesus has been consistently defined in relation to the disciples. They are explicitly told to "sit here" (26:36) and "remain here and watch with me" (26:38) while Jesus goes forward to pray.

Jesus then "fell prostrate" (literally, "on his face"). This accentuates the overwhelming effect of his profound distress and anxiety in view of his imminent death. From the depths of his anguished prostration Jesus commences his prayer with an address to God as "My Father." Throughout the narrative Jesus has been identified as the special "Son of God" (2:15; 3:17; 4:3, 6; 8:29; 11:25–27; 14:33; 16:16; 17:5). Now Jesus, in direct correspondence to the heavenly proclamations of God himself that "this is my beloved Son; with whom I am well pleased!" at both his baptism (3:17) and transfiguration (17:5), relies upon this unique sonship as he affectionately and respectfully begs God as "my" intimate and loving "Father" for deliverance from his approaching death.

Jesus prays, "If it is possible, let this cup pass from me." The deferential preface "if it is possible" (*dynaton*) comes from the mouth of the same Jesus who reminded his disciples that "for God all things are possible" (*dynata*, 19:26) and that "whatever you ask for in prayer with faith, you will receive" (21:22; see also 17:20). When Jesus introduces his earnest prayer with "if it is possible," he does so knowing and firmly believing that the God who is his loving "Father" is powerful enough to answer the prayer of his "beloved Son" for deliverance from death.

That Jesus ardently prays for his Father to let this "cup" (*potērion*) of suffering and death pass by him presents a shocking contradiction not only to his earlier assurance that the two sons of Zebedee would drink the "cup" (*potērion*) that Jesus "drinks" and thus share in his suffering and death (20:22–23) but also to the giving of the Passover "cup" (*potērion*) of his wine-blood, which all the disciples drank as a sacramental participation in his suffering and death in the previous b scene (26:27–28). In accord with his prior lament (26:38), Jesus' plea here for "this cup" to pass brings his deep dread and sorrow to a climax.

The dramatic tension between the divine necessity that Jesus suffer and die and his quite human dread of suffering and death is resolved through the very process of his praying as Jesus utters the words "but not as I will but as you will!" In thus submitting his own will to the sovereign will of his Father, Jesus shows how he is indeed God's obedient and "beloved Son." By so praying, he exemplifies the key characteristic of his new "family" of followers: "whoever does the will of my Father in heaven is my brother and sister and mother!" (12:50). For those he calls to follow him on his way to suffering and death, Jesus now demonstrates what it means to "think the things of God" rather than the "things of human beings" (16:23) and to "deny oneself" (16:24) in order to take up one's cross and follow him—namely, to deny one's own will in favor of God's sovereign and salvific will.

Jesus' acceptance of God's will over his own will in prayer, even though he knows and believes that God has the power to let this cup of suffering and death pass by him, develops his earlier teaching about prayer. Although disciples are to pray with faith in God's absolute power to grant their request (21:21–22; 18:19–20; 17:20), they must realize that God, although he possesses unlimited power, does not always choose to exercise that power to remove suffering and death. The will of God remains sovereign. But the Gethsemane prayer of Jesus illustrates how one can voice the deepest of human fears and concerns with firm faith that God can alleviate them and yet ultimately submit one's own will to God's sovereign will precisely in and through such prayer.

Jesus exhorts sleeping disciples to watch and pray (26:40–41). Returning to the three disciples after his prayer, Jesus "found them sleeping" (26:40) rather than awake and "watching" as he had commanded (26:38). This advances the theme of the disciples' separation from Jesus as developed in the previous a scene (26:30–35). Jesus' prediction of abandonment and denial prepared the reader for the disciples' temporary separation from him in accord with God's plan until after his resurrection and reunion with them in Galilee (26:31–32). But now the Gethsemane scene foreshadows and serves as a paradigm for the reader's situation of separation from Jesus after his resurrection and before his final, triumphant coming.

That Jesus finds the disciples sleeping is precisely what he had warned them against in his discourse preparing them for the time before his final coming: "Watch, therefore; for you do not know on which day your Lord will come. Be sure of this: if the master of the house had known the hour of the night when the thief was coming, he would have watched and not let his house be broken into. So too, you also must be prepared, for at an hour you do not expect the Son of Man will come" (24:42–44). After the parable of the ten virgins who fell asleep waiting for the bridegroom (25:1–12), Jesus exhorted the disciples, "Watch, therefore, for you know neither the day nor the hour" (25:13). The disciples' sleeping, then, refers not only to their inability to stay awake and "watch" during this critical time while Jesus prays but to their and the reader's potential failure to be prepared for Jesus' final coming by "sleeping" rather than "watching."

But the contrast with the previous a scene (26:30–35) becomes especially evident in Jesus' reproachful question to Peter as the representative for all the disciples: "So you could not watch with me for one hour?" (26:40). Jesus' reproach to Peter is in the second person plural (*ischysate*), indicating that it is directed not just to Peter but to the group of disciples. The failure of Peter and the other disciples to demonstrate their close bond of discipleship with Jesus by watching "with me" (*met' emou*, see also 26:38) stands in ironical contrast to the previous promises of Peter and the disciples not to desert Jesus (26:33, 35). That Peter cannot watch for even one hour with Jesus contradicts his prior boast that even if he must die "with you" (*syn soi*), he will not deny Jesus (26:35).

Developing his previous commands, Jesus now commands the disciples to "watch and pray" (26:41). His addition of the command to pray indicates the significance and power of his own praying. Now that he has prayed, he can command and empower his disciples likewise to pray:

> Sit here while I go over there and pray.
> Remain here and *watch* with me.
> He fell prostrate in *prayer*.
> *Watch* and *pray*.

That Jesus prays precisely while the disciples sleep and are unable to watch indicates that the prayer of Jesus is not only the model for the disciples to emulate in their prayer but is the basis or empowerment for their own praying. The sleeping disciples can now "watch and pray" only because Jesus has first successfully watched and prayed.

Jesus enjoins his disciples to watch and pray in order that they not "enter the test" (26:41), recalling how he earlier taught them to pray that God, "Our Father," not allow "us to enter into the test but to deliver us from the evil one" (6:13). The "test," "trial," or "temptation" (*peirasmon*) refers to God's final struggle with and conquering of the powers of evil, which is now reaching a crescendo with the suffering and death of Jesus. The dreaded "test" embraces not only this critical "hour" of Jesus' suffering and death but the future time of the disciples' own persecution, sufferings, and deaths (10:16–25; 24:9–13). Although the praying of the disciples will not guarantee the elimination of their sufferings and distress, the powerful prayer of Jesus has demonstrated how they, in and through his praying, can deny themselves and conform their wills to the sovereign will of God through their praying and thus withstand the terrible "test."[22]

The disciples need to watch and pray because of the fundamental and constant tension that "the spirit is willing but the flesh is weak" (26:41). In other words, although the "spirit," that part of the human person attuned to God and the spiritual, transcendent realm, is "willing" or "eager" to obey God's will, the "flesh," that part of the human person attuned to oneself and the earthly, limited, and mortal realm, is "weak" and thus disinclined to obey the will of God. This basic tension has been demonstrated by Peter and the disciples, whose "spirit" is willing to die with Jesus (26:35) but whose "flesh" prevents them from staying alert and watching. Jesus illustrates how to overcome this tension between "spirit" and "flesh" in and through prayer. In his prayer of lament Jesus, distressed and sorrowful over his imminent death, fully voiced his own concerns of the "flesh" as he begged his Father to let the cup of suffering and death pass by him. But in and through his prayer he allowed his "willing spirit" to predominate over the "weak flesh" as he submitted his own will to that of God (26:39).

Through repeated prayer Jesus fully accepts God's will (26:42). There is a notable progression in Jesus' submission to the will of his Father as he prays a second time:

> My Father, if it is possible, let this cup pass from me; but not as I will but as you will. (26:39)
>
> My Father, if it is not possible that this cup pass without my drinking it, your will be done. (26:42)

When Jesus prayed the first time, he left open the "possibility" (*dynaton*) that his Father's will might correspond to his own will not to drink the cup of suffering and death. But in his second prayer he realizes that it is "not possible" (*ou dynatai*) for him to escape drinking the "cup," and without any further mention of his own "will" totally resigns himself to the will of God: "Your will be done!" His repeated prayer thus enables Jesus to accept his Father's will even more fully and absolutely. With an exact echo of the "Our Father" prayer he taught his disciples, "your will be done" (*genēthētō to thelēma sou*, 6:10; 26:42), Jesus not only exemplifies how to pray but makes it possible for the disciples and the reader to accept and accomplish God's will on the strength of his prayer.

Jesus announces the arrival of his betrayer (26:43–46). When Jesus returns from praying a second time, he finds the disciples still "asleep, for their eyes were heavy" (26:43), further illustrating the weakness of their "flesh," unable to watch and pray. This continued inability of the disciples to stay awake and understand the significance of this critical time underlines and intensifies their stark contrast to the ardent and profound praying of Jesus. That they fail to watch and pray while Jesus continues to pray enhances the importance of the power of Jesus' prayer for them.

After he has prayed a decisive and definitive "third time" (26:44), Jesus returns to find his disciples still unable to stay awake, watch, and pray: "Are you still sleeping and taking your rest?" (26:45). Jesus then begins to illustrate how his praying has transformed him. Whereas he had begun praying that if it were possible God might allow the cup of his suffering and death to pass by him (26:39), now that he has totally submitted his own will to the sovereign will of God through prayer (26:42), he is able to proclaim with resolute acceptance, "Behold, the hour has arrived" (26:45). Continuing to demonstrate how his prayer has enabled him to overcome his fearful distress and deep sorrow over his approaching death, Jesus announces: "The Son of Man is betrayed into the hands of sinners." He thereby not only indicates his resolved recognition of the divine necessity of his suffering and death but climactically proclaims that his previous predictions are presently being fulfilled:

> The Son of Man is to be delivered/betrayed into the hands of men (17:22)
> The Son of Man will be delivered/betrayed to the chief priests and the scribes (20:18)
> The Son of Man will be delivered/betrayed to be crucified (26:2)
> The Son of Man is betrayed/delivered into the hands of sinners (26:45)

Now that he has completed his powerful prayer, Jesus' authoritative announcement of his betrayal sets in motion the events leading to his suffering and death.

Jesus' exhortation to the disciples, "Get up, let us go!" (26:46), indicates the powerful effect his prayer has in uniting them to himself, further developing the theme of the disciples' close union with Jesus in the previous b scene (26:26–29). Before he withdrew to pray, Jesus commanded his disciples to "sit here" and "remain here" while he prayed (vv. 36, 38). But after he has prayed, Jesus empowers his disciples to "get up" from their inert, sleeping position and enables them to "go" with him—"Let *us* go!" Now that Jesus has been strengthened through his prayer, he and his disciples can "go" together to play their respective roles in God's plan—the bewildered disciples to be "scattered" (26:31) and Jesus to be betrayed.

With the climactic exclamation "Behold, my betrayer has arrived!" (26:46), Jesus not only intensifies his announcement "Behold, the hour has arrived!" (26:45) but illustrates his determined readiness—now that he has submitted to God's will through prayer—to face his betrayer.

Jesus' special commemorative Passover meal in the previous b scene (26:26–29) gave his disciples, and by implication the reader, the opportunity of sharing in the salvific effects of his death (26:28) as they look forward to sharing in his triumphant meal in the kingdom of God (26:29). Now the b scene of Jesus' Gethsemane prayer (26:36–46) furthers this theme of union with Jesus as it enables his disciples and thus the reader to overcome, in and through their union with the powerful praying of Jesus, their inability to stay awake and "watch" for the "hour" of his triumphant coming (24:36–44). Within the network of intercalations in Matt 26:1–56, then, the Gethsemane scene brings to a climax the theme of solidarity with Jesus on his way to death as developed by the sequence of alternating b scenes (26:6–13, 17–19, 26–29, 36–46).

Jesus Is Arrested, Betrayed by Judas, and Abandoned by His Disciples (a^5 26:47–56)

> 47While he was still speaking, behold Judas, one of the Twelve, came,
> and with him a large crowd with swords and clubs, from the chief priests
> and elders of the people. 48His betrayer had arranged a sign with them,
> saying, "The man I shall kiss is the one; arrest him." 49Then immediately
> approaching Jesus, he said, "Hail, Rabbi!" and affectionately kissed him.
> 50Jesus said to him, "Friend, do what you have come for." Then approaching they laid hands on Jesus and arrested him.
>
> 51And behold, one of those with Jesus, stretching out his hand, drew
> his sword and, striking the high priest's servant, cut off his ear. 52Then
> Jesus said to him, "Put back your sword into its place, for all who take up
> the sword will perish by the sword. 53Do you think that I cannot call upon

my Father, and he will provide me now with more than twelve legions of angels? [54]But then how would the Scriptures be fulfilled that it must be done in this way?"

[55]At that hour Jesus said to the crowds, "Have you come out as against a robber with swords and clubs to capture me? Day after day I sat teaching in the temple, yet you did not arrest me. [56]But all this has happened that the writings of the prophets may be fulfilled!" Then the disciples all left him and ran away.

Jesus is betrayed by Judas and violently arrested (26:47–50). Concluding a narrative sandwich with the two previous scenes, Jesus' betrayal, arrest, and abandonment (26:47–56) not only contrasts with but also develops both the theme of union with Jesus in his prayer with his disciples (26:36–46) and the theme of separation from Jesus in his prediction of his disciples' abandonment (26:30–35).

With the immediate arrival of Judas, the contrast to the teacher-disciple bond Jesus has just strengthened by uniting the disciples more closely to him through his Gethsemane prayer begins. While Jesus "was still speaking," that is, precisely as he was announcing, "Behold, my betrayer has arrived!" (26:46), Judas, again designated as "one of the Twelve," reinforcing the terrible tragedy that it was one of Jesus' closest followers who betrayed him (26:14, 20–25), "came" (26:47) on the scene. That Judas arrives immediately in accord with Jesus' authoritative pronouncement accentuates Jesus' majestic control, in conjunction with God's plan, over the deceitful machinations of his enemies.

That Judas brings with him a "large crowd" armed "with swords and clubs" adds to the suspense by creating an expectation of a violent betrayal and possible resistance by Jesus and/or his disciples. The armed crowd accompanying Judas is from "the chief priests and elders of the people" (26:47), those Jewish leaders Judas has offered to assist (26:14–16) in their wicked scheme "to arrest Jesus by deceit and kill him" (26:5). But in so doing they are at the same time unwittingly fulfilling God's plan as continually predicted by Jesus (16:21; 17:12, 22–23; 20:17–19; 26:2, 24).

As "his betrayer," Judas had previously arranged a sign with the armed crowd, whereby he would "kiss" Jesus as the one they should seize (26:48). This false demonstration of affection underlines the treachery and tragedy of his betrayal, as he sadly abuses the close bond he enjoyed with Jesus as "one of the Twelve." Judas's command to "arrest" (*kratēsate*) the one he kisses indicates that it is his own betrayal that will enable the Jewish leaders to fulfill their desire to "arrest" (*kratēsōsin*) Jesus by deceit (26:4).

Immediately approaching Jesus, Judas greets him, "Hail, Rabbi!"

(26:49), recalling his earlier insincere "Surely it is not I, Rabbi" (26:25), the inadequate address that distinguished him as the betrayer from the rest of the disciples, who more appropriately addressed Jesus as their Lord (26:22). He then gives the signal for the arrest as he not only "kissed" him but "kissed him with affection," intensifying his tragic treachery (see 2 Sam 20:8–10; Prov 27:6).[23]

Not taken by surprise, Jesus, more Lord than Rabbi, counters Judas's traitorous gesture: "Friend, do what you have come for" (26:50). By addressing Judas as "friend" (*hetaire*), the same term used in the previous narrative by the landowner (20:13) and the king (22:12) to their subordinates, Jesus indicates his superiority over and detachment from this defector. By ordering him to proceed with his scheme, Jesus not only unmasks the deception disguised in his betrayer's greeting but exercises his sovereign control of the event. Once Jesus has given the command, "then" (*tote*), and only then, the armed crowd violently "laid hands" on him, proving themselves to be the "sinners" into whose "hands" the Son of Man is now betrayed in accord with Jesus' pronouncement (26:45). The crowd finally accomplishes the "arrest" the Jewish leaders have been intently plotting in their plan to destroy him:

> Seeking to arrest [*kratēsai*] him. (21:46)
> They consulted together to arrest [*kratēsōsin*] Jesus by deceit and kill him. (26:14)
> They laid hands on Jesus and arrested [*ekratēsan*] him. (26:50)

Jesus espouses God's will over violence (26:51–54). Suddenly the expected resistance comes not from Jesus but from "one of those with [*meta*] Jesus" (26:51), that is, one of the disciples Jesus has just joined closely "with" himself in the Gethsemane scene. In a defensive reaction to the violent laying of "hands" on Jesus by the crowd wielding "swords and clubs" (26:47), this disciple stretches out his "hand," draws his own "sword," strikes and cuts off the ear of an important member of the arresting crowd, the very "servant of the high priest," inflicting him with a painfully humiliating and disgraceful wound. But such violent retaliation exhibits a complete misunderstanding of Jesus' arrest. It clearly contradicts Jesus' pronouncement in the previous a scene (26:30–35) of what must happen: "I will strike the shepherd, and the sheep of the flock will be scattered" (26:31). That this disciple "strikes" (*pataxas*) the servant of the high priest with his "sword" indicates his futile resistance to the scriptural will of God (Zech 13:7), according to which Jesus (not the high priest's servant) is the "shepherd" whom God will metaphorically "strike" (*pataxō*) with suffering and death.[24]

But this retaliating disciple also misunderstands what it means to be a disciple "with" Jesus. In accord with his teaching against retaliatory violence (5:38–48), Jesus commands the disciple to put away his sword, because, according to the proverbially vicious circle of violent vengeance (Gen 9:6), "all who take up the sword will perish by the sword" (26:52). Jesus thus admonishes this disciple and all who would be a disciple "with" him to renounce violence rather than join those who, like the crowd who have taken up swords to arrest him, are destined for destruction.

The question Jesus then addresses to this avenging disciple, with its assertion that "my Father" could even now provide "twelve legions of angels" to rescue Jesus (26:53), develops the dynamics of the powerful prayer Jesus just uttered in the previous b scene at Gethsemane (26:36–46). Jesus' confident conviction that his Father could provide him with rescuing angels (see 4:11) illustrates how it would indeed be "possible" for Jesus to avoid the "cup" of suffering and death, if he, as God's beloved Son, insisted upon the powerful protection of "my Father" (26:39, 42). But Jesus' penetrating query, "How would the Scriptures be fulfilled that it must be done in this way?" (26:54), reinforces the total submission to his Father's will that he accomplished through his praying:

> Your will be done [*genēthētō*]. (26:42)
> It *must* be done [*genesthai*] in this way. (26:54)

Thus Jesus calls this disciple and all who would be his disciples to join him in subordinating themselves not to vengeful violence but to God's scriptural will in and through the power of Jesus' praying.

All disciples abandon Jesus (26:55–56). At that fateful "hour" of his betrayal as Son of Man in accord with God's will (26:45), Jesus makes his own nonviolent reply to the inappropriate violence exercised by the crowds who have arrested him (26:55). He indignantly and sarcastically inquires whether they mistake him for a "robber," since they have come out to capture him with "swords and clubs." The ironic implication is that the crowds rather than Jesus represent the real "robbers" who employ "swords and clubs" as weapons of unwarranted and unjust violence, an irony enhanced by Jesus' earlier denunciation of the Jewish leaders as the "robbers" who have degraded the Jerusalem temple into a "den of robbers" (21:13). The confused and misdirected crowds have been sent by real "robbers" (*lēstōn*) to violently capture one who is no "robber" (*lēstēn*).

The reproachful irony continues as Jesus proclaims that "day after day," that is, continually and in broad daylight, as he sat in the temple publicly "teaching," they had an obvious opportunity to arrest him, but they did not do so (26:55). Jesus' ironic rebuke recalls how the Jewish leaders, although they wanted to arrest and destroy Jesus, could not do so because of the crowds' favorable estimation of Jesus as a "prophet" (21:11, 46). Since they could not legitimately arrest Jesus while he was openly teaching the people (26:5), they must resort to treachery and violence in the secluded darkness of Gethsemane. Jesus thus sarcastically unmasks their ruthless deceit while exonerating himself as innocent and no "robber."

Jesus' climactic exclamation "But all this has happened that the writings of the prophets may be fulfilled!" (26:56) explains why the armed crowds sent by the Jewish leaders can only now arrest him. It is not that they have triumphed over Jesus, nor that he is a "robber," but that they are playing their role in fulfilling God's prophetic Scriptures. As soon as Jesus calls for "the writings of the prophets" to be fulfilled, "then" (*tote*), and only then, do the disciples oblige by running away and abandoning him (26:56). This advances the theme of separation from Jesus in the previous a scene (26:30–35), as the disciples fulfill Jesus' prediction in accord with a "writing" of the "prophet" Zechariah that they would all fall away from him and be "scattered" like "sheep of the flock" when the "shepherd" has been struck (Zech 13:7 in 26:31).

When the first disciples were called by Jesus, they admirably "left" behind their occupations, families, and everything to follow him. Now they all shamefully "leave" behind Jesus and thus renounce their discipleship:

> Immediately leaving [*aphentes*] their nets, they followed him. (4:20)
> Immediately leaving [*aphentes*] the boat and their father, they followed him. (4:22)
> Then Peter in reply said to him, "Behold, we have left [*aphēkamen*] everything and followed you". (19:27)
> Then the disciples all left [*aphentes*] him and ran away. (26:56)

That "all" the disciples fled further underlines the fulfillment of Jesus' previous prediction that they would "all" fall away from him (26:31) despite the spirited protests of "all" (26:35). It also stands in paradoxical contrast to the fact that "all" of them were invited to drink from the Passover cup of Jesus' wine-blood, to share the close bond of fellowship with Jesus on his way to suffering and death:

> Drink from it, all [*pantes*] of you (26:27)
> All [*pantes*] of you will fall away (26:31)
> Then the disciples all [*pantes*] left him and ran away (26:56)

Judas's action (26:48–49) climaxes both Jesus' prediction of betrayal (26:20–25) and Judas's offer of betrayal (26:14–16). The crowd too finally accomplishes the "arrest" (26:50) that the chief priests and the elders of the people have been seeking in their plot to destroy Jesus (26:3–4). Within the network of sandwiches in Matt 26:1–56, then, Jesus' betrayal, arrest, and abandonment (26:47–56) brings to a preliminary climax the theme of opposition to and separation from Jesus on the part of the Jewish leaders, Judas, and the disciples as developed by the sequence of alternating a scenes (26:1–5, 14–16, 20–25, 30–35, 47–56).

Summary

Through the intricate narrative structure of Matt 26:1–56 the reader experiences a succession of alternating scenes that form a network of intercalations involving, on the one hand, the theme of opposition to and separation from Jesus on his way to death and, on the other, the theme of close union with Jesus on his way to death. In the reader's experience of these alternating intercalations, the theme of intimate union with Jesus developed in the b scenes offsets and predominates the theme of opposition to and separation from Jesus developed in the a scenes. The succession of b scenes in contrast to a scenes repeatedly and progressively reassures the reader that despite the opposition to and separation from Jesus on his way to death by the Jewish leaders, Judas, and the disciples, Jesus will ultimately triumph over this because of the intimate bond that he has established and will continue to establish with those who follow him.

Despite the plot of the Jewish leaders and the betrayal of Judas, the reader is reassured that Jesus' anointing for burial will become part of God's saving activity to be commemorated in the proclamation of the gospel throughout the world. The preparation for and sharing of the Passover table fellowship between Jesus, the authoritative Teacher, and his special group of twelve disciples predominate the prediction of the betrayal of Jesus by one of the Twelve to reassure the reader that this unique Passover meal not only unites the disciples with the saving death of Jesus but promises them a share in the triumphant table fellowship with Jesus in the kingdom of "my Father." The reader is also reassured and encouraged by the promise of the disciples' future reconciliation with the risen Jesus and by his powerful Gethsemane prayer, which empowers the disciples and thus the reader to remain united with Jesus in their future encounters with opposition, suffering, and death in and through his prayer of submission to God's will.

NOTES

1. D. Senior, *The Passion Narrative According to Matthew: A Redactional Study*, BETL 39 (Leuven: Leuven University, 1975) 13–14.

2. "Son of Man" is the apocalyptic, messianic title Jesus alone uses to refer to himself throughout the narrative: 8:20; 9:6; 10:23; 11:19; 12:8, 32, 40; 13:37, 41; 16:13, 27–28; 17:9, 12, 22; 18:11; 19:28; 20:18, 28; 24:27, 30, 37, 39, 44; 25:31; 26:2, 24, 45, 64. Based on its background in Daniel 7, it refers to a transcendent figure who functions as the agent of God's kingdom and the leader of God's people. See. C. C. Caragounis, *The Son of Man: Vision and Interpretation*, WUNT 38 (Tübingen: Mohr-Siebeck, 1986).

3. BAGD, 614–15.

4. J. P. Heil, "Significant Aspects of the Healing Miracles in Matthew," *CBQ* 41 (1979) 283–84.

5. Jewish piety recommended almsgiving especially during the time of Passover, when many poor pilgrims were present; see John 13:29.

6. F. Lentzen-Deis, "Passionbericht als Handlungsmodell? Überlegungen zu Anstössen aus der 'pragmatischen' Sprachwissenschaft für die exegetischen Methoden," *Der Prozess gegen Jesus: Historische Rückfrage und theologische Deutung*, QD 112, ed. K. Kertelge (Freiburg/Basel/Vienna: Herder, 1988) 216–17.

7. LXX Exod 12:14 states in regard to the Passover: "This day shall be a memorial [*mnēmosynon*] for you, and you shall celebrate it as a feast to the Lord for all your generations; as a perpetual institution you shall celebrate it."

8. See the outline and explanation in chapter 1.

9. R. H. Gundry, *Matthew: A Commentary on His Literary and Theological Art* (Grand Rapids: Eerdmans, 1982) 522: "Judas Iscariot and Caiaphas, the treacherous disciple and the persecuting high priest, stand together."

10. LXX Zech 11:12: They paid (*estēsan*) my wages, thirty pieces of silver (*triakonta argyrous*). Matt 26:15: They paid (*estēsan*) him thirty pieces of silver (*triakonta argyria*). See J. P. Meier, *Matthew*, New Testament Message 3 (Wilmington: Glazier, 1980) 313.

11. Jesus' authoritative instructions to his disciples here recall his similar instructions to the two disciples sent to procure the animals for his entrance into Jerusalem in 21:1–11.

12. Matt 8:19; 9:11; 12:38; 17:24; 19:16; 22:16, 24, 36.

13. This is the last reference to Jesus as "teacher" (*didaskalos*) in Matthew. For the previous references to his "teaching," see Matt 4:23; 5:2; 7:28–29; 9:35; 11:1; 13:54; 21:23; 22:16, 33.

14. For previous acknowledgments of Jesus' sovereign "lordship" in Matthew, see 7:21–22; 8:2, 6, 8, 21, 25; 9:28; 10:24–25; 12:8; 14:28, 30; 15:22, 25, 27; 16:22; 17:4, 15; 18:21; 20:30, 31, 33; 21:3; 24:42.

15. On the concept of covenant, see J. Behm, s.v. *diathēkē*," *TDNT* 2.132–34; J. Unterman, s.v. "Covenant," *Harper's Bible Dictionary*, ed. P. J. Achtemeier (San Francisco: Harper & Row, 1985) 190–92.

16. Note the salvific and liberating effect of the "blood" of God's "covenant" in Zech 9:11: "As for you also, because of the blood of my covenant with you, I will set your captives free from the waterless pit."

17. J. Jeremias, s.v. *polloi*, *TDNT* 6.536–45.

18. Traditionally the Passover meal concluded with the singing of the "Hallel," Ps 113–18, which recalled God's liberation of Israel from Egypt and of the individual from death (Ps 116:1–9).

19. See "Jesus as the true King" in chap. 1.

20. See "Jesus as the Nazorean from Galilee" in chap. 1.

21. For a discussion of dramatic irony, see J. P. Heil, "Reader-Response and the Irony of Jesus before the Sanhedrin in Luke 22:66–71," *CBQ* 51 (1989) 273–74.

22. On the similar function of Jesus' praying in Luke, see L. Feldkämper, *Der betende Jesus als Heilsmittler nach Lukas*, Veröffentlichungen des Missionspriesterseminars St. Augustin bei Bonn 29 (St. Augustin, West Germany: Steyler, 1978) 224–50.

23. Note the intensification of affection in the progression from "I shall kiss" (*philēsō*, 26:48) to "he affectionately kissed (*katephilēsen*) him" (26:49). M. Zerwick and M. Grosvenor (*A Grammatical Analysis of the Greek New Testament* [Rome: Biblical Institute, 1974] 1.158) suggest the translation "he kissed him with every show of affection."

24. In Zech 13:7 a "sword" is the weapon that "strikes" the shepherd.

CHAPTER 3

The Innocent Jesus Dies as True King and Son of God (Matt 26:57—27:54)

Jesus Admits His Divine Sonship (Matt 26:57–75)

Peter Follows While Jesus Is Led to the High Priest (a[1] 26:57–58)

> 57Those who had arrested Jesus led him away to Caiaphas the high priest, where the scribes and the elders were assembled. 58Peter was following him at a distance as far as the palace of the high priest, and going inside, he was sitting with the servants to see the end.

Jesus is led to the high priest (26:57). The armed crowd who had violently captured Jesus (26:50) now lead him back to the Jewish leaders who had commissioned them to seize him (26:47). They bring him before the high priest Caiaphas, the highest ranking Jew and head of the Sanhedrin, the supreme Jewish tribunal. It was Caiaphas's servant who had been humiliated as one of Jesus' disciples severed his ear during the violent arrest (26:51). That the scribes and the elders have "assembled" (*synēchthēsan*) with Caiaphas to form the Sanhedrin recalls how the chief priests and elders of the people had earlier "assembled" (*synēchthēsan*) at the palace of Caiaphas to plot the deceitful arrest and death of Jesus (26:3–4). Now that he has been apprehended, Jesus stands before a gathering of the highest Jewish authorities, intent upon putting him to death. But Jesus had already authoritatively predicted that it would be precisely the elders, chief priests, and scribes who would deliver him to death in fulfillment of God's plan (16:21; 20:17–19).

Peter follows at a distance (26:58). Although all the disciples had left Jesus and run away after his arrest (26:56), Peter is still following him, but only "at a distance" (*apo makrothen*). With its allusion to LXX Ps 37:12, "My friends and my associates have drawn near and stand opposite me, and my companions stand at a distance [*apo makrothen*]," Peter's apprehensive following from afar contributes to the portrait of Jesus as the "suffering just one." Peter's distance from Jesus demonstrates how his discipleship is disintegrating. Although he "follows" Jesus, as he did when first called to be a disciple (4:18–20), he does not closely associate with his master. The contrasting positions of Peter and Jesus relative to the high priest create the suspense of this scene for the reader. Although Peter enters the palace of the high priest, rather than standing courageously with Jesus before the high priest he cautiously sits "with" the servants. At this point he is content with the posture of a spectator, merely watching, not yet participating in, the "end" (*telos*). Will Peter, the preeminent disciple who had boasted that he would die "with" Jesus (26:35), join his master on his way to death, as befits a true disciple (16:24), or deny him as Jesus predicted (26:34)?

Jesus Admits His Divine Sonship to the High Priest and Is Condemned to Death (b[1] 26:59–68)

> 59The chief priests and the whole Sanhedrin kept seeking false testi-
> mony against Jesus in order to put him to death, 60but they found none,
> though many false witnesses came forward. Finally two came forward and
> 61stated, "This man said, 'I have the power to destroy the sanctuary of God
> and within three days rebuild it.'"
>
> 62The high priest rose and said to him, "Have you no answer? What are
> these men testifying against you?" 63But Jesus remained silent. Then the
> high priest said to him, "I charge you under oath to the living God to tell
> us whether you are the Christ, the Son of God." 64Jesus said to him, "You
> have said it. But I tell you:
>
> From now on you will see 'the Son of Man seated at the right hand of
> the Power' [Ps 110:1]
> and 'coming on the clouds of heaven' [Dan 7:13]."
>
> 65Then the high priest tore his robes and said, "He has blasphemed!
> What further need have we of witnesses? Now you have heard the blas-
> phemy; 66What do you think?" They said in reply, "He is deserving of
> death!" 67Then they spat in his face and struck him, while some slapped
> him, 68saying, "Prophesy for us, O Christ, who is it that struck you?"

Jesus can destroy and rebuild God's sanctuary (26:59–61). To accomplish their wicked design of putting Jesus to death, the chief priests and the entire Sanhedrin flagrantly transgress a commandment of the Jewish law (Exod 20:16; Deut 5:20) as they kept seeking "false testimony" (*pseudomartyrian*, see 19:18; 15:19) against Jesus (26:59). This underlines the theme of the innocence of Jesus as the persecuted but faithful "just one" whom God will ultimately vindicate (Pss 27:12–14; 35:11; 37:32–33; 54:5–6).[1]

Frustrated in their attempt to find the false testimony needed to condemn Jesus to death, although many "false witnesses" do come forward, the Jewish leaders are finally presented with the apparently true testimony of "two" (26:60), the proper number of witnesses needed for the death sentence (Num 35:30; Deut 17:6; 19:15). These two witnesses testify that they have heard Jesus claim, "I have the power to destroy the sanctuary of God and within three days rebuild it" (26:61).

This bold accusation provokes the reader to reflect upon the profound theme of Jesus' relation to the temple in the previous narrative. While Jesus never explicitly claimed that he himself had the power "to destroy" (*katalysai*) the "sanctuary" (*naos*)—the building that contained the Holy of Holies as the place of God's unique presence and of the most important acts of worship, the very epitome of the special sacredness of the entire temple (*hieron*) complex—he did predict the utter destruction of all the impressive buildings of the temple (24:1): "There will not be left here a stone upon a stone that will not be thrown down (*katalythēsetai*)" (24:2). In so doing, Jesus had hinted at the inadequacy of the many magnificent buildings of the temple, including its central "sanctuary," as a permanent dwelling of God and locus of genuine worship.

In his earlier controversies with Jewish leaders, Jesus provocatively proclaimed that "something greater than the temple is here" (12:6) and that his ministry of compassion for human need accorded with the prophecy of Hos 6:6, that God desires "mercy" rather than the "sacrifice" performed in the temple (12:7; 9:13). After he arrived in Jerusalem and entered the temple, Jesus condemned it as being worthy of destruction for failing to achieve its purpose to be God's "house of prayer" (21:12–19). When these two witnesses transform Jesus' prediction of the entire temple's ultimate demise into the claim that he himself has the "power" to destroy the sacred "sanctuary" of the temple, they not only provide a damaging accusation toward Jesus' condemnation to death but present the reader with a new revelation of the profound power Jesus possesses over the heart and epitome of the entire temple complex.

The two true witnesses compound their accusation by attributing to Jesus the ridiculous boast that within "three days" he would "rebuild" the destroyed sanctuary. For the reader this boast proves to be a profound prophecy of the power Jesus will exercise through his death and resurrection. The "three days," an absurdly short period to rebuild the sanctuary, recalls the "third day" on which Jesus predicted that he would rise from the dead (16:21; 17:23; 20:19). It is through his death and resurrection, then, that Jesus will "build" (*oikodomēsai*, 26:61) a new and superior "sanctuary," constructed by the divine power manifested in his resurrection. This new "sanctuary," however, will not be another humanly made building but a divine construction, the new communal edifice God will erect upon the "cornerstone" of the risen Jesus. This had been indicated by Jesus' parable about the wicked tenants in which he revealed that by his death as God's Son he would become the "stone" rejected by the "builders" (*oikodomountes*, 21:42), the Jewish leaders in charge of the temple sanctuary, but whom God, by raising him from the dead, would make the "cornerstone" of a new edifice, the community of Jesus' followers (21:33–43). The power of Jesus' resurrection, then, is the power by which he will fulfill his promise that Peter will be the "rock" upon which "I will build" (*oikodomēsō*) my church (16:18).

As a new "sanctuary" this community will perform the authentic worship the old sanctuary failed to achieve. It will be a community characterized as God's familial household of genuine prayer (21:13), a community that prays with faith in God's limitless power to provide for his people (21:22), a community that practices compassion toward fellow human beings, the divine "mercy" that surpasses "sacrifice" performed in the temple sanctuary (9:13; 12:7). The true testimony of these two witnesses prompts the reader to probe the profound paradox that it is precisely through the death of Jesus, the aim of their accusation, that he will exercise the divine power of his resurrection to "build" a new, superior "sanctuary," the communal edifice of Jesus' followers, which will demonstrate that indeed "something greater than the temple is here" (12:6).

Jesus affirms his messianic divine sonship (26:62–64). The high priest rises and asks Jesus whether he has an answer for what these two witnesses are testifying against him (26:62). That Jesus "remained silent" advances his portrayal as the "suffering servant" of God (Isa 53:7) and the "suffering just one" (Pss 38:14–16; 39:10), who, although totally innocent, silently endures his accusers, willing to undergo the unjust death that is their aim, so that he can enable their accusation (26:61) to be revealed as a true prophecy fulfilled by his death and resurrection. Drawing out the implication that only the Messiah and Son of God has the divine power to destroy and rebuild the sanctuary, and invoking the oath taking Jesus abrogated for his followers (5:33–37), the high priest tries to force Jesus to answer: "I charge you under oath to the living God to tell us whether you are the Christ, the Son of God" (26:63). The high priest thus challenges Jesus to confirm, at the risk of being condemned to death, the earlier confession by Peter, "You are the Christ, the Son of the living God!" (16:16).

Refusing to participate in the high priest's oath, Jesus replies with the indirect affirmation "You have said it" (26:64), the same reply that indicated Judas's self-condemnation for his betrayal (26:25). Jesus thus turns the oath back upon the high priest, indicating that his own words have condemned him of putting God's Messiah to death. Through his affirmation of his true messianic identity, however, Jesus courageously accepts the death to which it leads. His admission that he is "the Christ, the Son of the living God," then, places him in sharp contrast to Peter, who, although he uttered this same confession, is now sitting and watching (26:58) rather than dying with Jesus as he had boasted (26:35).

Adding to the confession of his messianic divine sonship, Jesus valiantly proclaims his ultimate vindication and triumph not only to the high priest but to the whole assembly (and readers): "From now on you will see [second person plural] the Son of Man seated at the right hand of the Power and coming on the clouds of heaven" (26:64). It is as the transcendent messianic figure of the "Son of Man" that Jesus must suffer, die, and rise in accord with God's scriptural will (16:21; 17:9, 12, 22–23; 20:17–19, 28; 26:2, 24, 45). And it is as the "Son of Man" that Jesus, through his death and resurrection, will be exalted and vindicated in ultimate triumph with power over his enemies, with power to destroy and rebuild the sanctuary, and with power to come again in glory to establish the final salvation of the kingdom of God.

In conjunction with his previous revelation (22:41–46) that he is the messianic "lord" and Son of God to whom the Lord God says (22:44), "Sit at my right hand, until I place your enemies under your feet" (Ps 110:1), Jesus' promise that he will be "seated at the right hand of the Power" indicates his future vindication and triumph over the Jewish authorities now condemning him to death. That Jesus will be enthroned at the right hand of God, designated as the "Power" (*dynameōs*), reinforces his claim to possess the "power" (*dynamai*) needed to destroy and rebuild the sanctuary and thus to demonstrate as a true prophecy what the two witnesses voiced as an impossible boast (26:61). Moreover, recalling his prediction (24:30) that at the end of time "they will see 'the Son of Man coming on the clouds of heaven' with great power and glory" (Dan 7:13–14), Jesus assures his listeners that after his death and resurrection he will be enabled to "come on the clouds of heaven," equipped with divine power and glory to establish the kingdom of God's final and definitive salvation for his elect (24:31).

Jesus' fearless confession and bold proclamation to the high priest serve not only as a provocative instigation for his opponents to put him to death in accord with God's plan but also as an encouragement for those who would be his faithful followers to death (16:24), especially Peter, now timidly sitting and watching (26:58). Jesus' brave answer to the high priest further illustrates the strength he gained for himself and his disciples through his Gethsemane prayer to accept his death as the will of his Father (26:36–46). His courageous response models what he had advised his disciples regarding their future persecution: "When they deliver you up, do not worry about how or what you are to speak. It will be given you at that hour what you are to speak. For it will not be you who are speaking but the Spirit of your Father speaking through you" (10:19–20). Jesus' authoritative prediction to the high priest thus assures those who would be his followers of the assistance of God's power to lead them to ultimate vindication and triumph with him.

Jesus is condemned to death and abused (26:65–68). The high priest responds by dramatically "tearing his robes" (2 Kgs 18:37—19:4; Jdt 14:19), underlining the extreme offensiveness of Jesus' statements (26:65). The exclamations "He has blasphemed" and "Now you have heard the blasphemy" label Jesus' bold confession and proclamation with a serious charge—that is, a grasping infringement upon and blatant dishonoring of the sovereign power and authority of God (9:3; 12:31). The high priest's question "What further need have we of witnesses?" implies that the testimony of Jesus himself accords with that of the two witnesses, so that the Sanhedrin now has enough evidence to condemn Jesus to death. For the reader the high priest's confidence of not needing any more "witnesses" (*martyrōn*) ironically points to the need for Jesus' followers, especially the reluctant Peter (26:58), to confirm his testimony by giving "witness" (*martyrion*) to their persecutors and the nations of their faith as followers of Jesus (10:17–18).

In response to the high priest's question "What do you think?" (26:66), the Sanhedrin finally pronounces the desired death sentence, as they all pronounced him "deserving of death." Their unjust judgment of Jesus, who is totally innocent because of the truth of his powerful proclamations, as "deserving" or "guilty" of a crime punishable by death ironically confirms him as the innocently "suffering just one." It is precisely by condemning Jesus to death in order to destroy him and render him powerless that his opponents will enable him to exercise the divine power of his resurrection over death, triumphantly vindicating his unjust death (26:64) and empowering him to destroy and rebuild the new sanctuary within the "three days" of his resurrection from death (26:61).

The members of the Sanhedrin then contemptuously "spat" in his face and struck him (26:67), adding to the picture of Jesus as the suffering servant and just one to be vindicated by God (Isa 50:6). Their taunt "Prophesy for us, O Christ, who is it that struck you?" (26:68) brings this scene to an ironic climax. They mock Jesus' claim to be the "Christ" who can fulfill his "prophecies" to destroy and rebuild the sanctuary (26:61) and to be vindicated as the exalted Son of Man (26:64). But their harassing query "Who is it that struck [*paisas*] you" recalls how Jesus' prophecy that God will "strike" (*pataxō*) the "shepherd and the sheep of the flock will be scattered" (26:31) has already been fulfilled through his arrest and the disciples' desertion (26:50–56). The irony that it is ultimately God who has "struck" Jesus underlines how the Jewish leaders are unwittingly fulfilling Jesus' past prophecies. Their ironic mockery assures the reader of the fulfillment of Jesus' prophecies to rise from the dead with power to form a new community of authentic worship and to come again as the messianic Son of God and Son of Man with divine power to establish the final salvation of God's kingdom.

Peter Denies Jesus in the Courtyard of the High Priest (a^2 26:69–75)

> [69]Peter was sitting outside in the courtyard. One of the maids
> approached him, saying, "You also were with Jesus the Galilean." [70]But
> he denied it before all, saying, "I do not know what you are saying!"
>
> [71]As he went out to the gate, another girl saw him and said to those
> there, "This man was with Jesus the Nazorean." [72]But again he denied it
> with an oath, "I do not know the man!"
>
> [73]After a little while the bystanders approached and said to Peter,
> "Surely you too are one of them, for even your speech gives you away."
> [74]Then he began cursing and swearing, "I do not know the man!" And
> immediately a cock crowed.
>
> [75]Then Peter remembered the word Jesus had spoken, "Before the
> cock crows you will deny me three times." And going outside he wept
> bitterly.

Peter denies being with Jesus (26:69–70). Peter's cowardly denial of Jesus (26:69–75) not only contrasts with the b scene of the courageous confession of Jesus before the high priest (26:59–68) but also develops the previous a scene of Peter's separation from Jesus (26:57–58).

As Peter was still "sitting outside in the courtyard" rather than standing and dying with Jesus before the high priest, a maid identifies him as having formerly been in the company of Jesus: "You also were with Jesus the Galilean" (26:69). Whereas the high priest, the highest ranking Jewish male, confronted Jesus under oath with the extremely serious question of his identity as "the Christ, the Son of God" (26:63), the maid of the high priest, a female of considerably less authority, confronts Peter with the less serious question of his association with Jesus identified only as "the Galilean." Encountering Peter as having been "with" (*meta*) Jesus, the maid underlines for the reader Peter's abandonment of his special teacher-disciple bond to be "with" (*meta*) Jesus (26:18, 20, 29, 36, 38, 40).

Whereas Jesus had fearlessly affirmed his true messianic identity to the high priest (26:64), Peter cowardly "denied [*ērnēsato*] before all" his special association "with" Jesus: "I do not know what you are saying" (26:70). The seriousness of Peter's public denial had already been indicated by the earlier words of Jesus: "Everyone who acknowledges me before people, I will acknowledge before my Father in heaven. But whoever denies [*arnēsētai*] me before people, I will deny before my Father in heaven" (10:32–33).[2] Peter's denial of "knowing" what the maid is saying in linking him with Jesus functions as an ironic understatement for the reader. Although Peter was the one who had confessed Jesus to be "the Christ, the Son of the living God" (16:16), he truly does not "know" what is involved in being "with" Jesus as a disciple—namely, to "deny oneself" (*aparnēsasthō*) and follow with Jesus on his way to suffering and death (16:24). Despite his protesting promise that "I will not deny [*aparnēsomai*] you" even if he must "die with" Jesus (26:35), in denying his association with Jesus, harmlessly designated as the "Galilean," Peter is tragically refuting the discipleship he had with Jesus in Galilee.

Peter denies knowing Jesus (26:71–72). As Peter "went out to the gate," further distancing himself from Jesus, another girl confronts him before those present: "This man was with Jesus the Nazorean" (26:71). The more specific designation of Jesus as "the Nazorean" intensifies the drama. Peter is now accused of association with "the prophet Jesus from Nazareth" (21:11), the "Nazorean" consecrated from his infancy as God's special agent (2:23).[3]

In contrast to Jesus, who before the high priest avoided the "oath" (26:63) he forbade his followers to use (5:33–37), Peter "with an oath" utters a more direct denial of Jesus: "I do not know the man!" (26:72). Peter emphatically reinforces the ironic understatement of his first denial. Although he confessed the true identity of Jesus as God's messianic Son (16:16), Peter really does not "know" Jesus. He does not understand what the "man" Jesus has just confessed to the high priest and the Sanhedrin—namely, that he is the Christ and Son of God precisely because he suffers and dies as the "Son of Man" (17:12, 22; 20:18; 26:2, 24, 45) who will come again, exalted in final triumph (26:64). In not knowing the "man" Jesus, Peter does not understand his identity as the "Son of Man."

Peter denies being a disciple (26:73–74). After a little while the drama continues to mount as the whole group of bystanders confronts Peter with his discipleship: "Surely you too are one of them, for even your speech gives you away" (26:73). The ironic understatements of the accusations against Peter now reach their climax. Peter is much more than merely "one of them"; indeed, he is the first-called (4:18), preeminent leader and spokesman for all the disciples, the one who vehemently protested that he would be the exception to all others by dying with Jesus rather than denying him (26:33–35).[4] Even Peter's "speech" giving away his discipleship expresses an ironic double meaning. Not only does his Galilean dialect disclose his association with Jesus the Galilean (26:69) but his "speech" throughout the narrative, especially his confession of Jesus' messianic divine sonship (16:16) and his boastful promise to die with Jesus (26:35), distinguishes him as a special disciple.

Confronted with such incriminating evidence by the entire assembly of bystanders, Peter panics in cowardice as he "began cursing and swearing," decisively and definitively denying his discipleship for the third time, "I do not know the man!" (26:74). His vehement cursing and swearing compounds his previous use of an "oath" (26:72), continuing his contrast to Jesus, who refuses to comply with the oaths he prohibited (26:63). The repetition that he does "not know the man" reinforces the tragic irony that indeed Peter does not know what it means to be a disciple of "the man" Jesus, despite his promise to die with him. The immediate crowing of the cock signals the fulfillment of Jesus' prophecy that "this very night before the cock crows you will deny me three times" (26:34). Against the foil of the Sanhedrin's mockery of Jesus' power to "prophesy" (26:68), Peter's triple denial has confirmed it.

Peter remembers Jesus' prediction and weeps (26:75). After Peter recalls Jesus' prediction of his triple denial before the cock crows, he goes outside and weeps "bitterly," an expression of deep remorse indicative of his repentance. Although he has failed miserably as leader of the disciples to follow and die with Jesus, Peter's experience of Jesus' power to prophesy his triple denial provides the hope that he will likewise experience the fulfillment of Jesus' prediction of reconciliation with his deserted disciples in Galilee after he has been raised (26:32).

That Peter "went outside" to weep bitterly in repentance completes the development of his separation from Jesus in the previous a scene (26:57–58). His emphatic "going outside" (*exelthōn exō*, 26:75) directly reverses his prior emphatic "going inside" (*eiselthōn esō*, 26:58) to sit with the servants of the high priest. By "going outside" of the high priest's courtyard, Peter not only completes his desertion of Jesus but also dissociates himself from those "inside" the place where Jesus has been judged deserving of death. Although Peter has denied Jesus rather than die with him, he not only repents but has nothing to do with those unjustly putting Jesus to death.

The Innocent Jesus Admits His Kingship (Matt 27:1–14)

The Condemned but Innocent Jesus Is Led to Pilate (b^2 27:1–2)

> [1]Early in the morning all the chief priests and the elders of the people took counsel against Jesus to put him to death. [2]Then binding him, they led him away, and delivered him to Pilate, the governor.

Jewish leaders decide to have Jesus put to death (27:1). The Jewish leaders' deliverance of Jesus to Pilate (27:1–2) not only contrasts with the previous a scene of Peter's denial of Jesus (26:69–75) but also develops the previous b scene of the Jewish leaders condemning Jesus to death (26:59–68).

In contrast to Peter's repentance and emphatic withdrawal from those seeking Jesus' death (26:75), the Jewish leaders are still intent upon it. In the early morning all the chief priests and the elders of the people advance their devious plot in the previous b scene to find false testimony "against Jesus" (*kata tou Iēsou*) in order to unjustly "put to death" (*thanatōsōsin*, 26:59) the innocent one they have already judged "deserving" of "death" (*thanatou*, 26:66), as they now reach an official and definite decision "against Jesus" (*kata tou Iēsou*) "to put him to death" (*thanatōsai*, 27:1).

Jewish leaders deliver Jesus to gentile governor (27:2). Against the foil of Peter's "going outside" and away from his accusers (26:71, 75), the accusers of Jesus "bound" him and forcefully "led him away" (27:2). That they "delivered" him to the gentile Pilate, the Roman governor of Judea, continues their exact fulfillment of what Jesus had predicted:

> The Son of Man will be delivered to the chief priests and scribes, and they will condemn him to death, and deliver him to the Gentiles to be mocked and scourged and crucified, but on the third day he will be raised. (20:18–19)
>
> Then binding him, they led him away, and delivered him to Pilate, the governor. (27:2)

Ironically the same Jewish leaders who in the previous b scene had cruelly mocked Jesus' power to "prophesy" (26:67–68) now play their role in confirming it.

That Jesus has been led before a "governor" (*hēgemoni*) establishes him as a paradigm for his disciples (and readers), whom he warned of the same fate: "They will deliver you to courts and in their synagogues scourge you, and you will be led before governors [*hēgemonas*] and kings for my sake as a witness to them and to the Gentiles" (10:17–18).

Judas Repents Because of Jesus' Innocence (a^3 27:3–10)

> [3]Then Judas, his betrayer, seeing that he had been condemned, repented and returned the thirty pieces of silver to the chief priests and elders, [4]saying, "I have sinned in betraying innocent blood." They said, "What is that to us? You see to it." [5]Then throwing the pieces of silver into the sanctuary, he departed; and he went away and hanged himself.
>
> [6]But the chief priests, taking the pieces of silver, said, "It is not lawful to deposit these in the temple treasury, for they are the price of blood." [7]After taking counsel, they bought with them the potter's field as a burial place for foreigners. [8]Therefore that field is called the Field of Blood to this day. [9]Then was fulfilled what had been said through Jeremiah the prophet, "And they took the thirty pieces of silver, the price of the valued one on whom a price had been set by some of the sons of Israel, [10]and they gave them for the potter's field, just as the Lord directed me" [Zech 11:12–13].

A repentant Judas returns the money and hangs himself (27:3–5). Judas's repentance of betraying Jesus' innocent blood (27:3–10) not only contrasts with the previous b scene of the Jewish authorities leading the innocent Jesus to death (27:1–2) but also advances the previous a scene of Peter's repentance of denying Jesus (26:69–75).

In contrast to the relentless resolve of the Jewish leaders to deliver

Jesus to death (27:1–2), Judas, after witnessing their condemnation of Jesus, "repented" his betrayal of Jesus and returned the "thirty pieces of silver," the paltry price of the betrayal (26:15), to the chief priests and elders (27:3). His confession that "I have sinned in betraying innocent blood" (27:4) continues the portrayal of Jesus as the innocently suffering "righteous one." Judas' confession joins the "innocent blood" (*haima athōon*) of Jesus to the "blood" (*haimati*) of the prophets Jesus predicted the present Jewish leaders would shed, as did their ancestors (23:30). In shedding the "innocent blood" of the "prophet" Jesus (21:11, 46), the Jewish leaders are already beginning to fulfill Jesus' prophetic warning (23:35–36) that the responsibility for "all the righteous blood [*haima dikaion*] shed upon earth, from the blood of Abel, the righteous one, to the blood of Zechariah [a prophet] will come upon this generation." The juxtaposition of Judas's confession that "I have sinned" (*hēmarton*) with his recognition that Jesus' "blood" is innocent recalls that Jesus' "blood" will be poured out for many for the forgiveness of "sins" (*hamartiōn*) (26:28). Judas exemplifies the need that he and all other sinners have for the salvific forgiveness the innocent blood of Jesus will effect.

But the chief priests and elders refuse to sympathize with the repentance of Judas, as they reply, "What is that to us? You see to it" (27:4). Their desire to place all responsibility for the "innocent blood" of Jesus upon Judas rather than to accept it themselves stands in startling contrast to the previous b scenes (26:59–68; 27:1–2), in which they are so doggedly determined to put the innocent Jesus to death unjustly. Their failure to be moved by Judas's acknowledgment of Jesus' innocence illustrates Jesus' parable of the two sons (21:28–32): The first son refused to work in his father's vineyard but later "repented" (*metamelētheis*) and went (21:29). But even when the Jewish leaders saw tax collectors and prostitutes believing in John the Baptist and thus entering the kingdom of God, they did not "repent" (*metemelēthēte*) and believe him (21:31–32). Now, even after they have seen that Judas "repented" (*metamelētheis*), the recalcitrant leaders do not themselves repent.[5]

Judas, however, forces the Jewish leaders to take responsibility for the innocent blood of Jesus, as he flings the pieces of silver back to their source, the temple "sanctuary" (27:5) administered by the chief priests who paid them to him (26:14–15). That he "departed" and "went away" to hang himself advances the theme of withdrawal from the unjust death of the innocent Jesus developing in the a scenes. Just as Peter repented his denial and "went outside" (*exelthōn exō*) the place where the Jewish leaders were condemning Jesus to death (26:75), so Judas repented his betrayal and "departed" and "went away" (*apelthōn*) from the murderous

Jewish leaders. That Judas went away and "hanged himself," taking his own life rather than participate in the unjust taking of Jesus' life, indicates the extreme seriousness not only of his betrayal but of the Jewish leaders' deadly design for the innocent Jesus. Judas's suicide confirms Jesus' declaration that it would have been better if his betrayer had never been born (26:24). Like Ahithophel, the traitorous counselor of David (2 Sam 17:23), Judas, the traitorous disciple of Jesus, hanged himself in disgrace. But Judas did repent and confess his sin, so that he can ultimately receive the forgiveness to be effected for the sins of all by the innocent blood of Jesus (26:28).

Jewish leaders buy the Field of Blood (27:6–10). The chief priests' announcement that "it is not lawful" to deposit the silver pieces in the temple treasury because they are the "price of blood" (27:6) is drenched with irony for the reader. Their concern for what is lawful or proper for God's temple stands in ironic contrast to their blatant disregard for what was lawful when they sought false testimony (26:59) to put Jesus, God's messianic son, to death in the previous b scenes. They indict themselves as the ones who transformed the silver pieces into the "price of blood" and rendered them unworthy for the temple treasury when they paid Judas with them (26:15)! And their designation of the money as the "price" or "value" (*timē*) of "blood" begins their tragically ironic underestimation of the true "price" and "value" of Jesus' blood.

The chief priests' "taking counsel" (*symboulion labontes*, 27:7) to rid themselves and the temple of the price of Jesus' innocent blood ironically contrasts with the "counsel" the Jewish leaders "took" (*symboulion elabon*, 27:1) against Jesus to put him to death in the previous b scene. The dramatic irony heightens as they attempt to dispose of the blood money by purchasing "the potter's field as a burial place for foreigners" (27:7). In deeming the price/value of Jesus' blood as unworthy for the temple and fit only to buy an unclean burial place for unclean people, the Jewish leaders are unwittingly disclosing for the reader the true "value" and "price" of Jesus' innocent blood. They show the salvific "value" of Jesus' blood, which purchases a burial place for the "foreigners" or "strangers" (*xenois*) with whom Jesus identified himself: "I was a stranger [*xenos*] and you welcomed me" (25:35, 38, 43–44). They thus use the price/value of Jesus' blood ironically to perform the kind of hospitable and compassionate behavior toward foreigners that Jesus taught and exemplified (5:43–48; 8:5–13; 15:21–28). They also show the tragic "price" of Jesus' blood, which purchases a burial place for the "foreigners," who will replace the people of Israel in God's kingdom

(8:11–12; 21:43), because the Jewish leaders undervalued the blood of the one who was their messiah and Son of God.

Although the chief priests attempted to rid themselves of Jesus' blood money, its price and value continue to haunt them. The potter's field they purchase to dispose of the price of Jesus' blood is ironically called the Field of Blood "to this day" (27:8), an enduring reminder of both the tragic price and the salvific value of the innocent blood of Jesus, the "blood of the covenant to be poured out for many for the forgiveness of sins" (26:28).

But the Jewish leaders' tragic underestimation of the price and value of Jesus' blood is encompassed within God's scriptural program. Just as the tragedy of the shedding of the innocent blood of the infants in Bethlehem by the Jewish leader King Herod in his devious endeavor to eliminate Jesus "fulfilled what had been said through Jeremiah the prophet" (2:17), so now the tragedy of the Jewish leaders' futile attempt to dispose of the price and value of Jesus' innocent blood "fulfilled what had been said through Jeremiah the prophet" (27:9). Although most of the quotation to follow derives from Zech 11:12–13, it is appropriately attributed to Jeremiah (see Jer 19:1–11) as the prophet most closely associated with the tragic low point of Israel's history, the Babylonian captivity (see 1:11–12, 17), which resulted from their rejection of God and his prophets.[6] Jesus has already been insufficiently but aptly identified as "Jeremiah" (16:14), the preeminent prophet of persecution and tragic rejection by his own people.[7]

The chief priests fulfill the tragedy prophesied by Jeremiah (27:9–10) as they "took the thirty pieces of silver" (see 27:6), the paltry "price/value" (*timēn*) with which they, as "some of the sons of Israel," tragically "set a price" (*etimēsanto*) upon the Jesus they ironically reject as the truly "valued/priced" one (*tetimēmenou*) of God's people of Israel. In giving the silver pieces for the potter's field, which became the Field of the innocent "Blood" of the truly "valued/priced" one, they unwittingly do precisely as the Lord directed "me," the prophet. Just as Peter's denial in the previous a scene fulfilled Jesus' prophecy (26:69–75), so the Jewish leaders' futile and ironic endeavor to rid themselves of responsibility for the innocent blood of Jesus fulfills God's scriptural plan.

The Innocent Jesus Admits His Kingship to Pilate (b^3 27:11–14)

> [11]Jesus stood before the governor, and the governor questioned him, "Are you the King of the Jews?" Jesus said, "You say it." [12]And when he

> was accused by the chief priests and elders, he answered nothing. [13]Then Pilate said to him, "Do you not hear how many things they are testifying against you?" [14]But he did not answer him even one word, so that the governor wondered greatly.

Jesus admits his kingship to the governor (27:11). The admission by the innocent Jesus of his kingship to Pilate (27:11–14) not only contrasts with the previous a scene where Judas repents his betrayal of Jesus' innocent blood (27:3–10) but also advances the previous b scene where the Jewish authorities lead the innocent Jesus to death (27:1–2).

Against the foil of the Jewish leaders, "some of the sons of Israel," setting a "price" on their messiah in the previous a scene (27:9), Jesus, standing "before the governor" as a model for his disciples and the reader (10:17–18), courageously admits that he is "the King of the Jews" (27:11). In contrast to the chief priests and elders, who refuse responsibility for the innocent blood of Jesus by telling Judas, "You see to it" (*sy opsē*) (27:3–4), Jesus accepts responsibility for his "kingship" with its implications of sedition to the Roman government by telling Pilate, "You say it" (*sy legeis*).

Since Jesus has been bound as a prisoner, forcibly led away, and delivered by the leaders of the Jewish people to the Roman governor (27:1–2), treatment hardly appropriate for a "King of the Jews," Pilate's question is to be understood as an incredulous mockery of Jesus' kingship. Jesus' answer to Pilate's ridicule, "You say it" or "It is you who say so," throws the issue back on his questioner (see also 26:25, 64). Jesus does not claim the title "King of the Jews" for himself, but neither does he reject it. In what sense he is a "king" is to be determined by Pilate, the one who "says" it. The reader, who knows that Jesus is indeed "the King of the Jews" in the sense that he is the messianic Son of God through suffering, dying, and rising as the Son of Man (26:63–64), experiences the irony that Pilate is unwittingly playing his role in establishing how Jesus is truly "the King of Jews" precisely by mocking his kingship.[8]

But Jesus' affirmation of his kingship also develops the theme of the previous b scenes (26:59–68; 27:1–2). That Jesus now stands before "the governor" continues the deadly design of the Jewish leaders who delivered him to Pilate, "the governor" (27:2). Pilate's question to Jesus about whether he is the "King of the Jews" parallels and advances that of the high priest about whether he is the Christ, the Son of God, in the first b scene. Although in view of Jewish traditions about a Davidic, kingly messiah the two questions are nearly equivalent, Pilate's carries more political connotations of nationalistic rebellion. Jesus boldly affirms Pilate's question as he did that of the high priest:

> You have said it. (26:64)
> You say it. (27:11)

These questions and affirmations develop the theme of the b scenes, that of Jesus asserting and illustrating his more profound and innocent character precisely as the Jewish leaders are unjustly putting him to death.

The innocent Jesus refuses to answer his accusers (27:12–14). In ironic contradiction to their shunning the blame for the innocent blood of Jesus in the previous a scene (27:3–10), the chief priests and elders are now vehemently "accusing" Jesus in order to persuade the governor to put him to death (27:12). Pilate again questions Jesus, asking him if he wishes to reply to the charges the chief priests and elders have hurled against him. Pilate's query furthers the theme of the b scenes as it echoes that of the high priest during Jesus' trial before the Sanhedrin:

> The high priest rose and said to him, "Have you no answer? What are these men testifying against [*katamartyrousin*] you?" (26:62)
> Then Pilate said to him, "Do you not hear how many things they are testifying against [*katamartyrousin*] you?" (27:13)

That Jesus did not answer Pilate "even one word" (27:14), declining to defend himself against the false charges of the chief priests and elders, likewise echoes his silence to the high priest regarding the testimony against him:

> But Jesus remained silent (26:63)
> But he did not answer him even one word (27:14)

Jesus' reticence promotes his portrayal as the innocent "suffering servant" and "just one" (Isa 53:7; Pss 38:13–16; 39:10), who, although abandoned by friends and surrounded by false accusers, silently perseveres through persecution, faithfully relying upon God for his vindication.

Pilate "wonders greatly" (see Isa 52:14–15), amazed that one who affirmed he is "the King of the Jews" can remain defenselessly silent before his Jewish accusers. For the reader, however, the silence of Jesus further illustrates his true kingship. He is "the King of the Jews" precisely and paradoxically as the silently suffering servant and just one of God. Pilate's hesitant wonderment over Jesus and his accusers raises some doubt whether the Jewish leaders can persuade him to put Jesus to death. This b scene ends in suspense: Will Pilate side with the vociferous accusers or the silent Jesus?

Jesus Dies as God's Innocent, Royal Son (Matt 27:15–54)

Jewish People Accept Guilt for the Death of the Innocent Jesus (a^4 27:15–26)

> [15]Now on the occasion of the feast, the governor was accustomed to
> release to the crowd one prisoner whom they wished. [16]They had then a
> notorious prisoner called Jesus Barabbas. [17]So when they had assembled,
> Pilate said to them, "Which one do you want me to release to you, Jesus
> Barabbas or Jesus called Christ?" [18]For he knew that it was because of envy
> that they had delivered him.
>
> [19]While he was seated on the judicial bench, his wife sent him a
> message, "Have nothing to do with that righteous man, for I have suffered
> much over him today in a dream." [20]The chief priests and the elders
> persuaded the crowds to ask for Barabbas but to destroy Jesus. [21]Replying,
> the governor said to them, "Which of the two do you want me to release to
> you?" They said, "Barabbas!" [22]Pilate said to them, "What then shall I do
> with Jesus called Christ?" They all said, "Let him be crucified!" [23]But he
> said, "Why, what evil has he done?" But they cried out all the more, "Let
> him be crucified!"
>
> [24]When Pilate saw that he was gaining nothing, but rather that a
> tumult was beginning, he took water and washed his hands before the
> crowd, saying, "I am innocent of this man's blood. You see to it." [25]Reply-
> ing, all the people said, "His blood be upon us and upon our children!"
> [26]Then he released to them Barabbas, but Jesus he scourged and delivered
> to be crucified.

Pilate offers to release Jesus (27:15–18). The Jewish people's acceptance of the guilt for the death of the innocent Jesus (27:15–26) not only contrasts with but also develops the previous b scene of the innocent Jesus' admission of his kingship to Pilate (27:11–14). It also develops and contrasts with the previous a scene of Judas's repentance of his betrayal of Jesus' innocent blood (27:3–10).

Suspense builds when Pilate's customary Passover amnesty threatens to win the release rather than the death of Jesus, a death the Jewish leaders desired in the previous b scene (27:11–14). Since "the crowds" have been favorably attracted to the "prophet" Jesus (21:11, 46), it is likely that the "one prisoner" whom "the crowd" will want Pilate to release will be Jesus (27:15). That it was the occasion of the "feast" (*heortēn*) renews the suspense aroused by the Jewish leaders' desire not to arrest Jesus and put him to death during the Passover "feast" (*heortē*) in order to avoid a "tumult among the people" (26:5). Now that Jesus has been arrested and Pilate is drawing in "the crowd," will the Jewish leaders be able to avoid the tumultuous involvement of "the people" in their design to put Jesus to death?

The mention of another prisoner, one called "Jesus Barabbas" (27:16), adds to the suspense by introducing another candidate for release. As a "notorious" prisoner, the truly guilty Barabbas functions as the foil to the innocent Jesus. Once the crowd had officially "assembled," Pilate offers them an obviously lopsided choice between two who have in common only the name "Jesus"—the guilty Jesus Barabbas or the innocent Jesus "called Christ" (27:17). Pilate's designation of Jesus as the one "called Christ" begins to resolve the suspense of his "great wonderment" about Jesus that ended the previous b scene (27:14). He sides with the Jesus who affirmed that he is "the King of the Jews" (27:11) and "the Christ, the Son of God" (26:63–64), who is "called Christ" because he stands at the summit of Israel's salvation history (1:16–17).[9] Pilate offers "the crowd" the opportunity to accept as their true "Christ" the innocent Jesus whom their leaders want to kill.

Pilate's knowledge that it was out of "envy" for Jesus' popularity with the crowds (21:11, 15–16, 46) that the Jewish leaders "delivered" him (27:18; see 27:2) continues the theme of withdrawal from the guilt of the Jewish leaders in putting Jesus to death in the previous a scene (27:3–10). Judas separated himself from the guilty Jewish leaders when he realized that he had sinned in "betraying/delivering" (*paradous*) to them the "innocent blood" of Jesus (27:4–5). Now Pilate dissociates himself from the unjust jealousy of the Jewish leaders, as he tries to release the innocent Jesus, the "Christ," whom they have "delivered/betrayed" (*paredōkan*) to him out of envy (27:17–18).

Crowds demand that Pilate crucify the innocent Jesus (27:19–23). As Judas had pointed out the "innocent blood" of Jesus in the previous a scene (27:4), now, ironically, the wife of the gentile governor confirms through the divine guidance of a "dream" (see 1:20; 2:12, 13, 19, 22) that Jesus is indeed a "righteous man" (27:19).[10] But while she is warning Pilate, seated on the judicial bench, to have nothing to do with the Jewish leaders' conspiracy to put "that righteous man" to death, the chief priests and the elders are deviously persuading the crowds to request the release of Barabbas but the destruction of Jesus (27:20). This represents a critical turning point in the narrative. Although the Jewish leaders had been cautiously unwilling to involve the Jewish people, favorably impressed with the "prophet" Jesus (21:11, 46; 26:5), in their deadly design, Pilate's maneuver to release Jesus now forces them to try to sway "the crowds" against the enviably popular Jesus. Their change of tactics advances the theme, in the previous b scene (27:11–14), of their strategy to put Jesus to death. The "chief priests and elders" now seek to persuade not only the gentile governor (27:12) but their own people to destroy Jesus (27:20).

The drama mounts as Pilate poses the pivotal question to the crowds, "Which of the two do you want me to release to you?" (27:21). Their shocking answer, "Barabbas!" points to the stunning but tragic success of the Jewish leaders to persuade the crowds to undermine Pilate's ploy. Pilate then allows them to determine the fate of Jesus. The decision of "all" to "let him be crucified!" illustrates their tragic rejection of the Jesus who is truly their "Christ" (27:22). Following the lead of his wife that Jesus is a "righteous man" (27:19) as well as his own awareness (27:18), Pilate's plea, "Why, what evil has he done?" (27:23), underlines their unjust killing of a totally innocent Jesus. Nevertheless, they vociferously drown out Pilate's desperate appeal as they definitively reiterate, "Let him be crucified!"

All the people invoke Jesus' blood upon themselves (27:24–26). As Pilate realizes the futility of his stratagem to release the innocent Jesus, his concern that a "tumult was beginning" (*thorybos ginetai*, 27:24) signals for the reader the Jewish leaders' failure to prevent a "tumult" from "beginning" (*thorybos genētai*, 26:5) among the people. They have not been able to avoid the involvement of the Jewish people in the death of Jesus within the context of this salvific Passover feast.

Pilate then brings to a climax this a scene's development of the theme of withdrawal from responsibility for the unjust death of the innocent Jesus. That "he took water and washed his hands before the crowd" (27:24) serves as a symbolic protestation of Jesus' innocence with scriptural allusions (Deut 21:1–9; Pss 26:6; 73:13; Isa 1:15–16). According to the ritual recorded in Deuteronomy, when a corpse was found between two cities, "all the elders of the city nearest the corpse shall *wash their hands* over a heifer whose throat was cut in the wadi, and shall declare, 'Our hands did not shed this blood'" (Deut 21:6–7). When Pilate similarly declares, "I am innocent [*athōos*] of this man's blood [*haimatos*]" (27:24; see LXX 2 Kgs 3:28), he joins Judas's separation from the Jewish leaders' unjust killing of Jesus, when he confessed in the previous a scene, "I have sinned in betraying innocent blood [*haima athōon*]" (27:4). And when Pilate tells the crowd, "You see to it" (*hymeis opsesthe*), he ironically throws back upon the Jewish people the guilt for Jesus' blood that their leaders tried to shun when they told the repenting Judas, "You see to it" (*sy opsē*, 27:4).

In startling contradiction to the Jewish leaders' refusal to accept responsibility for the "price/value" of Jesus' innocent blood in the previous a scene (27:6–10), "all the people" (*laos*), representative of the entire covenant people of Israel (1:21; 2:6; 4:16, 23; 13:15; 15:8; 26:5), now solemnly accept full responsibility for the shedding of Jesus' blood: "His blood be upon us and upon our children!" (27:25; see 1 Sam 1:16; 2 Kgs 2:33; Jer 26:15). By boldly invoking the innocent "blood" (*haima*) of the "righteous man" (*dikaiō*, 27:19) Jesus, whom they regarded as a "prophet" (21:11, 46), "upon us" (*eph' hēmas*) and "upon our children," the Jewish people are fulfilling Jesus' prediction (23:35) that "upon you [*eph' hymas*] may come all the righteous blood [*haima dikaion*] shed upon earth, from the blood of Abel, the righteous one [*dikaiou*], to the blood of Zechariah" (a prophet). They even extend to future generations Jesus' warning that "all these things will come upon this generation" (*epi tēn genean tautēn*, 23:36), as they invoke his blood also "upon our children" (*epi ta tekna hēmōn*).

But by invoking "his blood" (*haima autou*) upon themselves and their future generations (27:25), the covenant people of Israel are also, ironically and unwittingly, invoking "my blood [*haima mou*] of the covenant to be poured out for many for the forgiveness of sins" (26:28). This advances the Matthean theme of the paradoxical "price" and "value" of the innocent blood of Jesus in the previous a scene (27:3–10). In calling down upon themselves the "blood" of Jesus, the Jewish people not only accept the tragic "price" for the unjust shedding of this blood, the loss of their special prerogative as a people to the kingdom of God which "will be given to a people that will produce its fruit" (21:43), but also play their paradoxical part in establishing the salvific "value" of Jesus' covenantal blood to effect the forgiveness of sins for all peoples (26:28). The Jewish people's acceptance of the full responsibility for the price/value of Jesus' blood ironically places them and all their future generations within the embrace of the forgiveness that the atoning blood of Jesus offers to all.

Although he has dramatically declared his innocence in the shedding of Jesus' blood, Pilate accedes to the wishes of the Jewish people as he releases Barabbas to them but scourges and delivers Jesus to be "crucified" (27:26), as they have demanded (27:22–23). Pilate finally "delivered" (*paredōken*) Jesus to the death the Jewish leaders sought when they "delivered" (*paredōkan*) him to Pilate out of envy (27:2, 18). But in so doing, Pilate plays his role in fulfilling God's salvific plan as predicted by

Jesus, that "they will deliver [*paradōsousin*] him to the Gentiles to be mocked and scourged and crucified" (20:19; 26:2).

While Dying, the Innocent Jesus Is Mocked as King and Son of God (b⁴ 27:27–44)

> [27]Then the soldiers of the governor took Jesus into the praetorium and assembled around him the whole cohort. [28]Then stripping him, they placed a scarlet military cloak around him. [29]And weaving a crown out of thorns, they placed it upon his head and a reed in his right hand. And genuflecting before him, they mocked him, saying, "Hail, King of the Jews!" [30]And spitting upon him, they took the reed and kept striking him on the head. [31]And when they had mocked him, they stripped him of the cloak, dressed him in his own clothes, and led him away to crucify him.
>
> [32]As they were going out, they found a Cyrenian named Simon; this man they compelled to carry his cross. [33]When they came to a place called Golgotha, that is, Place of the Skull, [34]they gave him wine mixed with gall to drink, but tasting it, he refused to drink. [35]After they had crucified him, they divided his clothes by casting lots. [36]Then they sat down and kept watch over him there. [37]And they placed over his head the written charge against him: This is Jesus, the King of the Jews. [38]Then two robbers were crucified with him, one on the right and one on the left.
>
> [39]Those passing by kept blaspheming him, shaking their heads [40]and saying, "You who would destroy the sanctuary and in three days rebuild it, save yourself, if you are the Son of God, and come down from the cross!" [41]Likewise the chief priests with the scribes and elders mocked him and said, [42]"He saved others; he cannot save himself! He is the King of Israel, let him come down now from the cross and we will believe in him! [43]He trusted in God, let him rescue him now if he wants him, for he said, 'I am God's Son.'" [44] In like manner the robbers crucified with him kept taunting him.

Gentile soldiers mock Jesus as King of the Jews (27:27–31). The mocking of the dying but innocent Jesus as King and Son of God (27:27–44) not only contrasts with but also develops the previous a scene of the Jewish people's acceptance of the guilt for the death of the innocent Jesus (27:15–26). It also develops and contrasts with the previous b scene of the innocent Jesus' admission of his kingship to Pilate (27:11–14).

In contrast to the emphatic refusal of Pilate, the governor, to participate personally in the killing of the innocent Jesus in the previous a scene (27:24), "the soldiers of the governor" readily take Jesus into the praetorium and "assemble" around him "the whole cohort" (27:27). This official "assembly" (*synēgagon*) of the "whole" (*holēn*) cohort of gentile soldiers who are to crucify Jesus parallels and complements not only the official "assembly" (*synēchthēsan*, 26:57) of the "whole" (*holon*) Sanhedrin to put Jesus to death (26:59) but also the official "assembly" (*synēgmenōn*, 27:17) of "all" (*pas*) the Jewish people, who accepted full responsibility for the shedding of Jesus' innocent blood (27:25).

Advancing the theme of the b scenes—namely, the "whole" Sanhedrin's ironical illustration of the innocent Jesus' true identity by putting him to death—the "whole" cohort of gentile soldiers performs a cruel parody of an official royal investiture of Jesus, further illustrating his true kingship. After stripping him of his own clothing, the soldiers place a "scarlet military cloak" around him, ironically clothing him as one of themselves and thus as their own King (27:28). The "crown" they weave out of "thorns" and place on Jesus' head serves not only as a mockery of a royal coronation but as a device for painful abuse. And the "reed" they place in his right hand parodies the ruler's scepter, a symbol of authority. Their ridicule of the royal reverence due Jesus by "genuflecting before him" ironically foreshadows and exemplifies the genuine reverence to be accorded him as the true King. Mimicking the regal acclamation accorded a Roman emperor or king, the soldiers salute Jesus with a ridiculing, "Hail, King of the Jews!" (27:29). These gentile soldiers' mockery of Jesus as the King rejected by his own Jewish people develops the irony of Pilate's mockery and Jesus' admission that he is "King of the Jews" in the previous b scene (27:11–14). For the reader the soldiers are unwittingly clothing, crowning, and hailing the true King not only of the Jews but also of the Gentiles.

The soldiers' "spitting upon him" is a gesture of deep contempt (Num 12:14; Deut 25:9) highly inappropriate for an authoritative ruler. And their "striking him on the head" with the "reed" (27:30) increases the pain inflicted by the crown of thorns, underlining the powerlessness of this "King" who helplessly suffers brutal abuse from the very "reed" or scepter with which he should be powerfully ruling. The gentile soldiers' contemptuous spitting and striking complements that of the Jewish leaders in the first b scene (26:67–68), promoting the paradox that Jesus is truly a King precisely by enduring abuse as the suffering servant and just one to be vindicated by God (Isa 50:6), rather than by displaying his own royal power.

After they have "mocked" him as King, the gentile soldiers "stripped" him of the "cloak" symbolic of royal status and honor and dress him again in his own ordinary clothing. They thus continue to reveal the radically new and profoundly paradoxical character of Jesus' kingship. The robe of royalty is quite inappropriate for Jesus, who shows himself to be a King unlike the gentile rulers and "great ones" who "lord" and "wield authority" over their subjects (20:25). That Jesus wears his own clothes rather than regal robes accords with the "greatness" he demonstrates as the "servant" King (20:26), who came as the Son of Man not "to be served but to serve and to give his life as a ransom for many" (20:28). As they then "led him away to crucify him" (27:31), the gentile soldiers begin to discharge the demand of the Jewish people in the previous a scene that he be "crucified" (27:22–23). The unhesitating determination of Pilate's soldiers contrasts with Pilate's own great wonderment at the defenseless "King of the Jews" in the previous b scene (27:14). But they will establish the innocent Jesus as the true "King of the Jews" precisely and paradoxically in and through his rejection, ridicule, suffering, and death (27:31).

The innocent Jesus is crucified as King of the Jews (27:32–38). That the soldiers crucifying Jesus "compelled" a certain Cyrenian named Simon, a Diaspora Jew from the city of Cyrene on the Mediterranean Sea in northern Africa, "to carry his cross" (*hina arē ton stauron autou*) makes this Simon, in the absence of the disciples, a substitute model of discipleship (27:32). Although forced, this Simon literally illustrates what Jesus demands of a disciple: "If anyone wishes to come after me, let him deny himself, take up his cross [*aratō ton stauron autou*] and follow me" (16:24). That they must "compel" Simon to carry the cross underscores the disciples' total abandonment of Jesus (26:56). "Simon" of Cyrene is forced to carry the cross in the absence of "Simon" called and named Peter by Jesus in Galilee (4:18; 10:2; 16:16–17; 17:25), the leader of the disciples who vowed to die with Jesus (26:35). Whereas Simon of Cyrene was "compelled" to carry the cross, the reader has been summoned to follow Jesus freely on his way of suffering and death by denying self and willingly taking up the cross.

They come to the place of crucifixion called "Golgotha," whose translation as "Place of the Skull" projects the ghastly aura of death (27:33). That they give him "wine mixed with gall" furthers the portrayal of Jesus as the suffering just one, who in the midst of shame and insults inflicted by foes is given "gall" and "vinegar" (Ps 69:20–22). That Jesus refuses to drink the drugged wine accords with his promise to "never again drink of the fruit of this vine until that day when I drink it new in the kingdom of my Father" (26:29). Jesus thus declines the drugged wine in order to "drink" and fully experience the "cup" of suffering and death willed for him by God (26:39, 42; 20:22–23) as the way to the establishment of the final and triumphant banquet of God's kingdom (27:34). After the soldiers crucify Jesus, they contribute to his portrait as the suffering just one when they "divided his clothes by casting lots" (Ps 22:19) to determine what each should take. Crucified as the suffering just one of God, Jesus dies utterly alone and forsaken, not only abandoned by his closest followers but bereft even of his own clothing (27:35).

That the soldiers "sat down" and "kept watch" over the crucified Jesus not only inserts a sense of expectancy for the reader but advances the irony of Jesus' kingship as they become his royal "guards" (27:36). The "written charge" that they place over the head of the innocent Jesus furthers the profound irony of establishing his true identity by putting him to death. They reveal that truly "this is *Jesus*," the one who is now saving his people from their sins (1:21) by shedding his blood (26:28), and the one who is the true "King of the Jews" precisely by being unjustly crucified (27:37).

The innocent Jesus, who was forcibly arrested as if a "robber" (*lēstēn*, 26:55), is now crucified in a mock royal enthronement as "King" between two "robbers" (*lēstai*, 27:38). These two robbers, presented as the royal attendants of the enthroned Jesus, "one on his right and one on his left," serve as substitute disciples for James and John, the sons of Zebedee, whose mother had requested that they "sit one at your right and one at your left" (20:21) in the "kingdom" of Jesus after promising to "drink the cup" of suffering and death that Jesus will drink (20:22) but who are now sadly absent. Disciples rather than "robbers" should be dying with Jesus (26:35) in order to participate in his "kingdom." By crucifying Jesus as a mock "King" between two "robbers," the soldiers are ironically enthroning him as the true "King of the Jews," since Jesus had earlier indicated that the Jewish leaders responsible for the inauthentic worship in the temple are the real "robbers" (*lēstōn*, 21:13). The two "robbers" thus ironically represent the Jewish leaders whose true and revolutionary "King" is the unjustly crucified Jesus (27:38).

Jews mock Jesus as King of Israel and Son of God (27:39–44). That those passing by "blasphemed" him while "shaking their heads" (27:39) continues the portrayal of Jesus as the suffering just one who is scorned by his accusers as they "shake their heads" at him in contempt (Pss 22:8; 109:25; Lam 2:15). Their mockery of Jesus' apparent powerlessness furthers the profound irony presented by their crucified King. They taunt him to "save himself" by coming down from the cross in order to demonstrate that he is truly the "Son of God" (see 4:1–11), as he confessed at his trial before the high priest in the first b scene (26:63), and to demonstrate that he can fulfill the boast attributed to him at that trial (26:61)—namely, that he has the "power" to "destroy" the temple "sanctuary" and "rebuild it in three days" (27:40).

In challenging him to "save himself" by coming down from the cross, his taunters are pointing the reader to the paradox that it is precisely by remaining on the cross and losing his life that Jesus will save it. This accords with Jesus' pronouncement that "whoever wishes to save his life will lose it, but whoever loses his life for my sake will save it" (16:25). By remaining on the cross and enduring the powerlessness of crucifixion, Jesus as the suffering just one will be raised from the dead by God "on the third day" (16:21; 17:23; 20:19) and thus demonstrate his divine power to destroy indeed the old "sanctuary" and erect a new one, the spiritual and communal "sanctuary" of authentic worship of God constituted by the followers of the risen Jesus, God's Son and "cornerstone" (21:42).

The "chief priests with the scribes and elders," the full and official assembly of those Jewish leaders who perpetrated the death of the innocent Jesus (26:57, 59), now bring their opposition to a climax as they intensify the ridicule of the passers-by (27:41). Their jeers express the profound paradox that although Jesus "saved others, he cannot save himself!" (27:42). Indeed, although Jesus has "saved" others throughout the narrative by teaching, healing, and exorcising, he cannot "save" himself from death because only God can and will save him by raising him after he has died. But that God will save him as he remains on the cross "to give his life as a ransom for many" (20:28; 26:28) means that he will "save" not only himself but "many" (= all) others in a more profound and definitive sense.

They then derisively dare Jesus to prove that he is truly the "King" not only of the "Jews," a sociopolitical community, but of "Israel," the chosen people of God, by coming down "now" from the cross. Then they will believe in him (27:42). This brings this b scene's development of the kingship of Jesus, introduced in the previous b scene (27:11–14), to its apex. When he stood before the gentile governor, Jesus courageously but evasively affirmed that he was the "King of the Jews" (27:11). The soldiers of the gentile governor then mockingly but truly clothed and hailed Jesus as the "King of the Jews" (27:29). Precisely by crucifying the innocent Jesus as the suffering just one, they revealed the profound truth of the "charge" against him—namely, that indeed "this is Jesus, the King of the Jews" (27:37). Now this full assembly of Jewish leaders complements and climaxes the gentile soldiers' establishment of Jesus' true kingship as they mockingly but ironically acknowledge the profound truth that "he is the King of Israel!"[11]

The reader sees irony here precisely because Jesus proves he is worthy of belief as the true King of Israel with power to save himself and all others by remaining on the cross and refusing to save himself from the death that is God's will.

The Jewish leaders then mock Jesus as the suffering just one put to death by his opponents precisely to test his trust in God's vindication: "He trusted in God, let him rescue him now if he wants him, for he said, 'I am God's Son'" (27:43; see Ps 22:9; Wis 2:18–20). They scoff at the trust Jesus as Son has placed in God as his Father, especially evident in his Gethsemane prayer (26:36–46). Their taunt for God to rescue him now if he "wants" him mocks God's own previous proclamations that Jesus "is my beloved Son, with whom I am well pleased" (3:17; 17:5). But the reader knows that Jesus will be vindicated for his trust as God's Son not by being rescued from death on the cross but by being raised from the dead and by coming again in glory as the Son of Man (26:64). With its reference to Jesus' admission to the high priest that he is "the Christ, the Son of God" (26:63) in the first b scene, their mockery of his claim to be "God's Son" brings the paradoxical theme of the b scenes (26:59–68; 27:1–2, 11–14, 27–44) to its climax: In and through their rejection and unjust execution of the innocent Jesus, the Jewish leaders ironically establish and demonstrate his profound identity as their true Christ, King and Son of God.

That even the "robbers" who were crucified with Jesus were scornfully taunting him "in the same manner" (27:44) underlines their association with the Jewish leaders as the real "robbers" (21:13), who are unjustly putting Jesus to death. Their abuse adds a finishing touch to the cruel mockery of Jesus, who is totally abandoned by his followers and despised, reviled, and mocked from all sides—by gentile soldiers, by anonymous passers-by, by the full assembly of Jewish leaders, and even by the robbers crucified with him.

The Death of the Innocent Jesus Vindicates His Divine Sonship (a^5 27:45–54)

> 45From the sixth hour darkness came over the whole land until the
> ninth hour. 46About the ninth hour Jesus cried out in a loud voice, "*Ēli,
> Ēli, lema sabachthani?*" that is, "My God, my God, why have you forsaken
> me?"
>
> 47Some of those standing there heard it and said, "This one is calling
> for Elijah." 48Immediately one of them ran and took a sponge, filled it with
> vinegar, placed it on a reed, and gave it to him to drink. 49But the rest said,
> "Wait, let us see if Elijah comes to save him!"
>
> 50But Jesus cried out again in a loud voice and gave up his spirit. 51And
> behold, the veil of the sanctuary was split in two from top to bottom. The
> earth was shaken, rocks were split, 52tombs were opened, and many bodies
> of the holy ones who had fallen asleep were raised. 53And coming forth
> from the tombs after his resurrection, they entered the holy city and
> appeared to many.

> [54]When the centurion and those with him who were keeping watch over Jesus saw the earthquake and the things that happened, they were greatly awed, saying, "Truly this was the Son of God!"

Jesus cries out in prayer (27:45–46). The vindication of Jesus' divine sonship at his death (27:45–54) not only contrasts with but also develops the previous b scene of the mocking of the dying but innocent Jesus as King and Son of God (27:27–44). It also develops and contrasts with the previous a scene of the Jewish people's acceptance of the guilt for the death of the innocent Jesus (27:15–26).

Now the crucified Jesus along with the whole earth is enveloped for three hours in an ominous and deathly darkness (27:45). During Jesus' crucifixion, from the "sixth hour" (noon) a "darkness" came over "the whole land [earth]" and lasted until the "ninth hour" (3:00 P.M.). That this mysterious "darkness" occurs at midday, endures for three hours, and covers the "whole land [earth]" indicates that it is an extraordinary, supernatural phenomenon brought on by God himself as a sign foreshadowing the end of the world (see 24:29). According to Amos 8:9 God himself promised to cause such a darkness on the end-time "day of the Lord": "'On that day,' says the Lord God, 'I will make the sun go down at noon, and cover the earth with darkness in broad daylight.'" Such supernatural darkness during Jesus' crucifixion characterizes his death as a preliminary event of God's end-time with significance for the whole world. The darkness counters the taunts, in the previous b scene (27:41–44), that presumed God's indifference to Jesus' crucifixion.

Jesus, "about the ninth hour" (3:00 P.M.) cries out in a "loud voice," quoting a Semitic (Hebrew-Aramaic) version of the first words of Psalm 22, a lament of the "suffering just one": "My God, my God, why have you forsaken me?" (27:46). The reporting of Jesus' words in Semitic along with their translation adds realism and rhetorically reinforces the great importance of his cry. Having endured God's silent "abandonment," symbolized by the dismal "darkness" God has caused instead of rescuing him from excruciating death at the hands of reviling accusers, Jesus begs for the reason "why" or "for what purpose" (*hinati*) God has "forsaken" him. Although indicative of his experience of intense anguish as he dies radically alone and without divine intervention, Jesus' cry is not one of despair but is the lamentful prayer of the suffering just one, uttered with complete confidence and total trust in his God. Expressing his deep personal relationship of faith in God, Jesus addresses him twice as "my God." And with confidence in his Father's sovereign plan for him, he calls out for God to refute the ridicule of his trust as God's Son in the previous b scene (27:43) by disclosing the purpose of Jesus' abandonment to death.

Bystanders wait to see if Elijah will save Jesus (27:47–49). Based upon a resemblance in sound between the Hebrew address "my God" (*Ēli*) in Jesus' cry and the name of the revered prophet "Elijah," some of the bystanders who hear it distort Jesus' lamentful prayer of trust in God into a plea for Elijah to rescue him: "This one is calling for Elijah" (27:47). In order to prolong Jesus' life, one of the bystanders offers him a drink from a sponge filled with vinegar and placed on a reed (27:48). By so doing he unwittingly contributes to the portrait of Jesus as the suffering just one whose reviling foes gave him "vinegar to drink" (Ps 69:22).

But the rest of the bystanders do not want him to delay or interfere with a possible miraculous rescue of Jesus. Their derisive desire to see if Elijah will "save" him (27:49) advances the malicious mockery of Jesus' divine power to "save" others and to be "saved" himself by God in the previous b scene:

> Save [*sōson*] yourself, if you are the Son of God, and come down from the cross. (27:40)
> He saved [*esōsen*] others; he cannot save [*sōsai*] himself. (27:42)
> He trusted in God, let him rescue him now if he wants him. (27:43)
> Wait, let us see if Elijah comes to save [*sōsōn*] him. (27:49)

By twisting his lamentful prayer of trust into a mocked plea for rescue, the bystanders continue to illustrate their stubborn blindness to the divine necessity of Jesus' death as the suffering just one. They do not understand that Jesus is exemplifying his teaching that salvation comes from the God who will ultimately "save" those who entrust themselves completely to him (19:25–26; 24:22) and that whoever wishes to "save" his life will lose it (16:25) and whoever perseveres to the end "will be saved" (10:22; 24:13).[12] The irony is that not even Elijah can rescue Jesus, because as Jesus himself stated, "Elijah has already come, and they did not recognize him but did to him whatever they pleased" (17:12–13). In the person of John the Baptist (3:4; 14:1–12) Elijah had already come and suffered the same fate Jesus is now suffering in accord with God's will.

Saints are raised at the death of Jesus (27:50–53). Demonstrating that he rather than the mocking bystanders has control of his death, Jesus repeats the loud cry of his prayer of lamentful trust in God and finally "gave up his spirit" (27:50), freely and obediently giving his life back to God as the suffering just one. In response to Jesus' death and as a beginning to the answer of "why" God has abandoned him to death, the "veil" or curtain hanging in the temple sanctuary "was split" by God (divine passive) in two pieces "from top to bottom," in other words, totally and irreparably destroyed from heaven downward (27:51).

This destruction of the sanctuary veil, symbolic of the entire temple cult, indicates the termination of the old temple "sanctuary" that Jesus had judged inadequate as the place of God's presence and authentic worship (21:12–17) and points to the advent of the new, superior "sanctuary." The tearing of the sanctuary veil, indicative of the entire temple's demise (23:38; 24:1–2), begins to fulfill the first part of the prophecy attributed to Jesus by the two witnesses at his trial before the Sanhedrin and to contradict the mockery of his powerlessness on the cross in the previous b scene:

> This man said, "I have the power to destroy the sanctuary of God and within three days rebuild it." (26:61)
> You who would destroy the sanctuary and in three days rebuild it. (27:40)
> And behold, the veil of the sanctuary was split in two from top to bottom. (27:51)

By his death on the cross in apparent weakness, Jesus demonstrates his power to destroy the old temple sanctuary and opens the way for his rebuilding of a new one.

A spectacular chain reaction of events continues God's vindication of Jesus' trust in him as his Son and suffering just one: The earth "was shaken" by God (divine passive), which causes the rocks to be "split" (divine passive) (27:51), which in turn enables the tombs, made and sealed with rocks, to be "opened" (divine passive), so that many bodies of the "holy ones" who had fallen asleep in death were "raised" (divine passive) from them (27:52; see Ezek 37:1–14; Dan 12:2). After Jesus' own resurrection these "holy ones" entered the "holy city" of Jerusalem and appeared to many (27:53).[13]

The resurrection and appearance of the many holy ones not only indicates that Jesus' death and resurrection inaugurates the end-time general resurrection of the dead but also develops the theme of the Jewish people's acceptance of responsibility for the "price" and "value" of Jesus' "blood" in the previous a scene (27:15–26). When the whole Jewish people invoked upon themselves and their children the "innocent" (27:4) and "righteous" (27:19) blood of the "prophet" (21:11, 46) Jesus (27:25), they began to fulfill Jesus' prediction that upon them would come the guilt for all the "righteous blood" shed upon earth, from the blood of Abel, the "righteous one," to the blood of Zechariah, a prophet (23:35), because they shed the blood of Jesus just as they, like their ancestors (23:30), shed the blood of the "righteous ones" (23:29), "prophets," "wise men," and "scribes" that God sends them (23:34). The "tombs" (*mnēmeia*) from which the holy ones are raised and come out (27:52–53) include the "tombs" (*mnēmeia*) the Jewish leaders built and adorned for the "righteous ones" and "prophets" whom they murdered (23:29). The resurrection of the "holy ones" signifies God's vindication for the Jewish people's unjust killing not only of his righteous ones, prophets, wise men, and scribes numbered among the "holy ones" but also of Jesus, his prophet and suffering righteous one.

That the resurrected "holy ones" enter the "holy city" of Jerusalem and "appear to many" after Jesus' resurrection (27:53) continues the vindicating testimony against the Jewish people's acceptance of guilt for the unjust shedding of Jesus' blood (27:25), as indicated in Jesus' lament over this most holy of Jewish cities for rejecting him just as it killed the holy ones sent by God: "Jerusalem, Jerusalem, you who kill the prophets and stone those sent to you, how many times I wanted to gather your children together, as a hen gathers her young under her wings, but you were unwilling!" (23:37). The triumphant "appearing" of the holy ones to the "many" in the holy city of Jerusalem not only testifies against those who have killed Jesus and the other prophets and holy ones God sent them but also encourages those who dare to follow in the footsteps of the suffering just ones God vindicates by raising from the dead.[14]

But the resurrection and appearance of the many holy ones also advances the theme of the Jewish people's ironical underestimation of the salvific "value" of Jesus' blood that they have invoked upon themselves (27:25). By shedding the innocent "blood" of Jesus they played their paradoxical part in effecting the salvific value of Jesus' "blood of the covenant to be poured out for many [*pollōn*] for the forgiveness of sins" (26:28). Now that the blood of Jesus has been poured out in his death, it has the life-giving, salvific effect of raising the "many [*polla*] bodies" of the holy ones from the dead, so that they bear witness of God's salvific vindication to the "many" [*pollois*] to whom they appear (27:53).

Gentile soldiers confess Jesus' divine sonship (27:54). The suspense aroused when the soldiers "sat down and kept watch over [*etēroun*] him there" (27:36) is now resolved as the centurion and the soldiers with him who "were keeping watch" (*tērountes*) over the dying Jesus saw the earthquake and the other spectacular "things that happened" at his death (27:54). In sharp contrast to the previous b scene, these gentile soldiers refute the mockery of Jesus' divine sonship by both the passers-by and the Jewish leaders:

> Save yourself, if you are the Son of God, and come down from the cross. (27:40)
>
> He trusted in God, let him rescue him now if he wants him, for he said, "I am God's Son." (27:43)
>
> They were greatly awed, saying, "Truly this was the Son of God." (27:54)

The soldiers' climactic confession illustrates God's vindication of the trust Jesus has placed in him as his Son by remaining on the cross. By proclaiming, "Truly this [*houtos*] was the Son of God," these gentile soldiers not only contradict the bystanders' misunderstanding that "this [*houtos*] one is calling for Elijah" (27:47) but also transform their own mockery of the crucified Jesus in the previous b scene that "this [*houtos*] is Jesus, the King of the Jews" (27:37) into a profession of faith in the crucified Jesus' profound identity. Their confession thus confirms that of Jesus himself before the high priest in the first b scene, when he admitted he was "the Christ, the Son of God" (26:63–64).

But the gentile soldiers' dramatic confession of Jesus' divine sonship also brings to its apex the theme of withdrawal from the Jewish leaders' unjust killing of Jesus in the a scenes (26:57–58, 69–75; 27:3–10, 15–26, 45–54). Whereas, in the previous a scene (27:24, 26), Pilate declared his "innocence" in the Jewish plot to put Jesus to death yet delivered him to be crucified, his soldiers' confession of faith in Jesus demonstrates their astounding conversion—from mocking, abusing, scourging, and crucifying (27:27–37) Jesus to vindicating him as the innocent Son of God.

These Gentiles' profession of faith in Jesus stands in keen contrast to the whole Jewish people's rejection of Jesus when they invoked upon themselves the responsibility for Jesus' blood in the previous a scene (27:25). These Gentiles further illustrate the ironical "price" the Jewish people pay for shedding the valuable blood of Jesus. Their confession qualifies them as representatives of the people to whom the kingdom of God will be given when it is taken from the Jewish people because of their rejection of Jesus (21:43). Through their confession of faith in Jesus, the gentile centurion and those with him become members of the new, communal "sanctuary" of authentic worship that Jesus has the power to "build" (26:61; 27:40) through his resurrection now that his death has pointed to God's destruction of the old sanctuary (27:51).

The climactic confession of Jesus' divine sonship by these gentile soldiers confirms the confession by God himself, by the disciples, by Peter, and by Jesus:[15]

> This is my beloved Son, with whom I am well pleased (3:17)
>
> Truly, you are the Son of God (14:33)

You are the Christ, the Son of the living God (16:16)
This is my beloved Son, with whom I am well pleased (17:5)
I charge you under oath to the living God to tell us whether you are the Christ, the Son of God (26:63)
Truly this was the Son of God (27:54)

Summary

Through the complex narrative structure of Matt 26:57—27:54 the reader experiences a progression of contrasting scenes that interweave two themes: (1) In the b scenes the Jewish leaders who unjustly execute the innocent Jesus ironically establish him as the true messianic King and Son of God; (2) in the a scenes those who withdrew from his unjust death confirm Jesus' innocence and profound identity. The succession of b scenes presents the reader with the tragic but inspiring model of Jesus as the innocently suffering just one, who, through complete trust in God, patiently endures rejection and death from his own people. The progression of a scenes presents the reader with the models of the conversion that is possible and necessary in order to recognize and accept Jesus' profound identity as God's suffering just one.

Against the foil of Peter's cowardly denial of Jesus but implicit repentance, the reader is encouraged by Jesus' brave affirmations of his identity in the face of the Sanhedrin's deadly rejection. In contrast to the Jewish leaders' deliverance of Jesus to the gentile governor Pilate for an unjust death, the explicit repentance of the disciple Judas assures the reader of the salvific value the Jewish leaders' shedding of Jesus' "innocent blood" will have.

Although Pilate's gentile soldiers as well as the Jewish leaders cruelly mock the apparent powerlessness of the crucified Jesus' kingship and divine sonship, the dramatic conversion of the soldiers convinces the reader that Jesus is indeed God's messianic royal Son precisely and paradoxically because the whole Jewish people brought upon themselves the tragic "price" as well as the salvific "value" of Jesus' innocent blood.

NOTES

1. J. Gnilka, *Das Matthäusevangelium: Kommentar zu Kap. 14,1—28,20 und Einleitungsfragen*, HTKNT 1/2 (Freiburg/Basel/Vienna: Herder, 1988) 426.

2. D. Senior, *The Passion of Jesus in the Gospel of Matthew* (Wilmington: Glazier, 1985) 100–101.

3. See "Jesus as the Nazorean from Galilee" in chap. 1.

4. F. J. Matera, *Passion Narratives and Gospel Theologies: Interpreting the Synoptics Through Their Passion Stories* (Mahwah, N.J.: Paulist, 1986) 103.

5. The similarity of Judas's repentance to that expressed by the same verb in Matt 21:28–32 plus his confession of sinfulness demonstrates that his repentance is full and genuine, against those who (like O. Michel, s.v. *metamelomai, TDNT* 4.628) devalue Judas's "repentance" as only "remorse" or merely a change of heart, since the term *metanoein* is not used.

6. R. H. Gundry, *The Use of the Old Testament in St. Matthew's Gospel*, NovTSup 18 (Leiden: Brill, 1967) 122–27; D. J. Moo, *The Old Testament in the Gospel Passion Narratives* (Sheffield: Almond, 1983) 189–210; D. Senior, *The Passion Narrative*, 343–97.

7. The identification of Jesus with Jeremiah is unique to Matthew, who exploits the tragic associations of this prophet to characterize the destiny of Jesus (2:17; 16:14; 27:9).

8. See "Jesus as the true King" in chap. 1.

9. See "Jesus as the Christ" in chap. 1.

10. R. Gnuse, "Dream Genre in the Matthean Infancy Narratives," *NovT* 32 (1990) 97–120.

11. See "Jesus as the true King" in chap. 1.

12. See "Jesus as Savior" in chap. 1.

13. "Holy city" here refers to the earthly rather than heavenly Jerusalem, as in 4:5.

14. R. D. Witherup, "The Death of Jesus and the Raising of the Saints: Matthew 27:51–54 in Context," SBLASP 26 (1987) 581.

15. See "Jesus as the Son of God" in chap. 1.

CHAPTER 4

The Authority of the Risen Jesus Prevails Through Witnesses of His Death, Burial, and Resurrection (Matt 27:55—28:20)

Women Followers Witness Jesus' Death and Burial (Matt 27:55–61)

Women Followers From Galilee Witness the Death of Jesus (a[1] 27:55–56)

> [55] There were there many women, looking on from a distance, who had followed Jesus from Galilee, ministering to him. [56]Among them were Mary Magdalene and Mary the mother of James and Joseph, and the mother of the sons of Zebedee.

Galilean women watch the death of Jesus from a distance (27:55). The presence at Jesus' death of the Jewish women from Galilee complements that of the gentile centurion and those with him (27:54). Whereas the group of gentile men represents recent converts to faith in Jesus based on witnessing his death in Jerusalem, the group of Jewish women, "who had followed Jesus from Galilee" (27:55), represents faithful followers of Jesus from the origin of his ministry. The use of the adverb *there* (*ekei*), as the women are introduced, "there were *there* many women," expressly links these Jewish women with the gentile centurion and those with him as witnesses to Jesus' death. The Jewish women from Galilee thus serve as substitutes for the male disciples of Jesus, "all" of whom "left him and ran away" (26:56) after he was arrested, as he had predicted in fulfillment of the Scriptures (26:31, 56).

The mother of absent disciples was there (27:56). That two of these women, the "mother" of James and Joseph and the "mother" of the sons of Zebedee (27:56), are identified by their relation to male characters reminds the reader of the absence of all male disciples and underlines the women's role as their substitutes. The mention of the mother of the sons of Zebedee, who had earlier proudly asked Jesus to give her sons positions of importance in his kingdom (20:20–21), particularly points up the tragic absence of two of the brothers Jesus first called to be disciples (4:21–22) and key members of his special group of Twelve (10:2; 17:1; 26:37). The reader is thus assured that despite the absence of all male disciples from Galilee, women followers related to them witnessed Jesus' death.[1]

Although the presence of the Jewish women complements that of the gentile men, their silence and passivity stand in sharp contrast to the exuberant proclamation of the centurion. Whereas the gentile men's "seeing" (*idontes*) of "the earthquake and the things that happened" produced a confession of Jesus' divine sonship (27:54), the Jewish women's circumspect "looking on" (*theōrousai*) from a distance reduces them, who had "ministered" to Jesus while following him from Galilee, to helpless witnesses looking on in strange silence (27:55). This stark contrast indicates that this scene of the women's witness (27:55–56) serves not only as the conclusion to the death scene (27:45–54) but also as the beginning of a new tension and suspense for the reader: Why do these Jewish women, who have witnessed the same events that resulted in the dramatic confession by the gentile men, remain surprisingly silent? What further role will the women play in contrast to them?

Because Jesus predicted his passion, death, and resurrection "on the third day" (16:21; 17:22–23; 20:17–19), and especially because the resurrection of Jesus has already been anticipated at his death (27:53), the reader does not expect the narrative to end with the death scene. As substitute disciples who have witnessed Jesus' dramatic death, the Jewish women are uniquely qualified to witness and participate in the events involving Jesus' resurrection. Their silent and passive witness of Jesus' death has thus created a new tension the reader expects to be resolved.

A Disciple From Arimathea Buries Jesus and Departs (b[1] 27:57–60)

> [57]When it was evening, there came a rich man from Arimathea, Joseph by name, who also had become a disciple of Jesus. [58]This man approached Pilate and asked for the body of Jesus. Then Pilate ordered it to be handed over. [59]Taking the body, Joseph wrapped it in clean linen [60]and laid it in his new tomb that he had hewn in the rock. Then rolling a huge stone across the entrance of the tomb, he departed.

A disciple receives Jesus' body from Pilate (27:57–58). A "rich man" (*plousios*), in contrast to the passivity of the "many women" (27:55), "came" (*ēlthen*) on the scene in the evening (27:57). Whereas the women are "from Galilee," the origin of Jesus' ministry, the rich man named Joseph is "from Arimathea." In contrast to the women who "had followed" (*ēkolouthēsan*) Jesus from Galilee, Joseph, in addition to being rich, "had become a disciple" (*emathēteuthē*) of Jesus.[2] That Joseph is both a rich man and a disciple strikes the reader as shockingly incongruous in view of what Jesus had earlier told his disciples: "Amen I say to you, it will be difficult for a rich man [*plousios*] to enter the kingdom of heaven. Again I say to you, it is easier for a camel to pass through the eye of a needle than for a rich man [*plousion*] to enter the kingdom of God" (19:23–24).

Nevertheless, Joseph's staus as a "rich" disciple enables him to request and receive the body of Jesus from Pilate (27:58), which neither the other male disciples who have fled (26:56) nor their substitutes, the women who are helplessly passive (27:55–56), are in a position to do.

The disciple buries Jesus and departs (27:59–60). Although the women had "ministered" to Jesus while following him from Galilee, it is Joseph who ministers to Jesus by burying him. He performs a service appropriate to a "disciple," that of properly burying his master, as the disciples of John the Baptist had buried their master (14:12). And so, in contrast to the women who look on passively as Jesus dies (27:55–56), Joseph personally carries out the burial of Jesus as he himself wraps the body in clean linen (27:59), lays it in his own new tomb, and rolls the huge stone to close the tomb and complete the burial. After solemnly performing his duty as a disciple, he "departed" from the scene (27:60).

The personal activity of Joseph in burying Jesus underlines for the reader the reality and significance of Jesus' death. By laying Jesus' body in his own new "tomb" (*mnēmeiō*), which he had hewn in the "rock" (*petra*, 27:60), Joseph places Jesus in the same realm of the dead from which the many bodies of the "holy ones who had fallen asleep" were raised at the death of Jesus: "The earth was shaken, the rocks [*petrai*] were split, the tombs [*mnēmeia*] were opened" (27:51–52). The resurrection of these many dead saints is based upon the resurrection of Jesus (27:53), who has been buried into the same realm of the dead. By burying Jesus in a rock-hewn tomb, Joseph has thus placed him in solidarity with the many saints who have died. The scene of Jesus' burial by Joseph of Arimathea, then, points the reader not only back to the death scene (27:45–54) to realize the reality and significance of Jesus' death but also forward to the expected resurrection of Jesus (27:53).

Mary Magdalene and the Other Mary Sit Facing the Tomb of Jesus (a² 27:61)

> [61]But there was there Mary Magdalene and the other Mary, sitting in front of the tomb.

The two named Mary remain at the tomb (27:61a). As the final scene of the first narrative sandwich, Mary Magdalene and the other Mary sitting in front of Jesus' tomb (27:61) not only contrasts with the b scene of the disciple Joseph's burial of Jesus (27:57–60) but also develops the a scene of the Galilean women's witnessing of Jesus' death (27:55–56).

Although Joseph admirably performed the reverent service of burying Jesus, after he rolled a huge stone across the entrance of the tomb, "he departed" (*apēlthen*, 27:60).[3] Once again the narrative is bereft of male disciples (see 26:56). In contrast to the absence of Joseph and all other male disciples, the two women named "Mary" from Galilee remain present at the tomb to function once again as substitute disciples (27:61a).

The two women sit expectantly in front of the tomb (27:61b). The scene of Mary Magdalene and the other Mary "sitting" there facing the "tomb" (*taphou*, 27:61b),[4] the locus of the expected resurrection of Jesus (27:53) "on the third day," as he had predicted to his disciples (16:21; 17:22–23; 20:17–19), also advances the motif of the silent and passive presence of the women at the death of Jesus in the first a scene (27:55–56). But now the "many women" have narrowed to two. Whereas "there were there [*ēsan de ekei*] many women" as witnesses to the death (27:55), "there was there [*ēn de ekei*] Mary Magdalene and the other Mary" as witnesses to Jesus' burial (27:61). These two women named Mary (the "other Mary" is the mother of James and Joseph, 27:56) are no longer described in relation to male characters.[5] They function not only as substitutes for absent male disciples but also as faithful witnesses to the death and burial of Jesus in their own right. They assure the reader of a continuity of reliable witnesses to both the death and burial of Jesus.

The silent and passive posture of the two Marys, "sitting [*kathēmenai*] in front of the tomb," reminds the reader of the similar posture of the soldiers in the previous narrative. After the soldiers had crucified Jesus (27:35), they "sat down" [*kathēmenoi*] and "kept watch over him there" (27:36). This vigilant "sitting" of the soldiers before the crucified Jesus placed them in a position to witness the marvelous events that happened upon his death (27:50–53), which led to their confession of his divine sonship (27:54). Similarly the vigilant "sitting" of the two women before the tomb of Jesus places them in a position to be witnesses of the anticipated resurrection of Jesus (27:53). The "sitting" of these two women in front of Jesus' tomb continues the aura of expectancy aroused by the silence and passivity of the women as they viewed Jesus' death (27:55–56). Prepared by the dramatic outcome of the soldiers' expectant sitting, the similar expectant sitting of the women alerts the reader to the significant role these women will play—as faithful witnesses to both the death and burial of Jesus—in the expected narration of Jesus' resurrection.

Jewish Leaders Try to Thwart Jesus' Resurrection (Matt 27:62—28:4)

The Chief Priests and Pharisees Receive Pilate's Permission to Seal the Stone and Guard the Tomb (b² 27:62–66)

> 62The next day, which is after the day of preparation, the chief priests and the Pharisees assembled before Pilate, 63saying, "Sir, we remember that this imposter while still alive said, 'After three days I will be raised up.' 64Give orders, then, that the tomb be secured until the third day, lest his disciples come and steal him and tell the people, 'He has been raised from the dead.' Then this last deception will be worse than the first." 65Pilate said to them, "You may have a guard; go secure it as you know how." 66They went and secured the tomb, sealing the stone with a guard.

Jewish leaders would prevent theft of Jesus' body (27:62–64). The chief priests and Pharisees receiving Pilate's permission to seal the stone and guard the tomb of Jesus (27:62–66) not only contrasts with the previous a scene of the two women sitting at the tomb (27:61) but also develops the previous b scene of Jesus' burial by a disciple (27:57–60).

This scene advances the theme of true authority over the dead body of Jesus begun by his burial in the previous b scene (27:57–60). First, the notice that the burial took place on the "evening" of the day of Jesus' death (27:57) progresses to the notice that it is now the "next day, which is after the day of preparation" (27:62). This unusual way of referring to the Sabbath as the day "after" (*meta*) the "day of preparation" serves to mark pointedly the second day in the three-day period between the death and the predicted resurrection of Jesus "on the third day" (16:21; 17:22–23; 20:17–19). The reader may also perceive a deeper meaning in this subtle reference to the day of Jesus' burial as the day of "preparation" (*paraskeuēn*)—namely, that Jesus' burial is the necessary "preparation" for his expected resurrection "on the third day" after his death.

Before Joseph buried Jesus, he received Pilate's official authorization to take the body, as "Pilate ordered [*ekeleusen*] it to be handed over" (27:58). Similarly the Jewish leaders ask for Pilate to exercise his authority to "order [*keleuson*] the tomb to be secured until the third day" (27:64) so as to prevent the fraudulent fulfillment of the promise of "this imposter" that "after three days I will be raised up" (27:63) through the theft of his body by his disciples. But the Jewish leaders' alarming conjecture that "his disciples" may steal the body of Jesus from the tomb in order to proclaim a false resurrection (27:64) sounds ridiculous to the reader, who knows of the total abandonment (26:56) and departure (27:60) of all the disciples as well as the notable passivity of their female substitutes (27:55–56, 61).

The negative posture of the Jewish leaders toward the tomb of Jesus conflicts with the positive posture of the faithful women toward the tomb in the previous a scene (27:61). Whereas the chief priests and Pharisees, after recalling Jesus' prediction of resurrection after "three days" (27:63) and receiving Pilate's permission to secure the "tomb" (*taphon*) until the "third day" (27:64),[6] attempt to prevent a fraudulent proclamation of Jesus' resurrection by securing the "tomb" (*taphon*) against theft (27:66), the faithful women sit in front of the "tomb" (*taphou*, 27:61), properly positioned to witness the fulfillment of Jesus' promise of resurrection "on the third day" (16:21; 17:22–23; 20:17–19).

Pilate grants a guard for the tomb (27:65–66). Although Pilate grants the Jewish leaders authorization to guard the tomb, he does so in a skeptical way (27:65). While Pilate had the legitimate authority to grant the dead body of Jesus to Joseph for burial, he does not have the authority to guarantee the Jewish leaders the prevention of Jesus' resurrection. Pilate's dissociation of himself from the futile attempt of the Jewish leaders is grammatically indicated by his use of the middle voice in the imperative "secure" (*asphalisasthe*) it, which means "secure" the tomb with the connotation of "yourself" or "in your own interests."[7] His dissociation from their dubious endeavor is further underlined by his additional words, "as you know how" or "as best you can" (*hōs oidate*, 27:65). As Pilate had earlier separated himself from guilt for the death of the innocent Jesus so that it fell upon the Jewish people swayed by their leaders (27:24–25), so now he separates himself from the vain attempt of the Jewish leaders. They must accept the responsibility and use their own "authority" for their foolish scheme to thwart Jesus' resurrection.

There is a further notable progression from the burial in the previous b scene. After Joseph laid the body of Jesus in his rock-hewn tomb, he closed and secured the tomb by rolling a huge "stone" (*lithon*) across the entrance (27:60). Now the Jewish leaders want to reinforce this burial in their design to prevent Jesus' resurrection, as they themselves seal the "stone" (*lithon*) with the guard granted by Pilate (27:66). Thus a conflict involving authority has emerged for the reader—namely, the dubious authority of the Jewish leaders to prevent Jesus' resurrection versus the reliable authority of Jesus' promise and God's power to raise him from the dead (27:63).

Mary Magdalene and the Other Mary Come to See the Tomb (a^3 28:1)

> [1]After the Sabbath, as the first day of the week was dawning, Mary Magdalene and the other Mary came to see the tomb.

It is the third day after Jesus' death (28:1a). Mary Magdalene and the other Mary coming to see Jesus' tomb (28:1) not only contrasts with the previous b scene of the Jewish leaders' sealing the stone of the tomb with a guard (27:62–66) but also advances the theme of these two women's faithful witness of Jesus' burial in the previous a scene (27:61).

In contrast to the chief priests and Pharisees, who secured Jesus' tomb (27:66) on "the next day" (27:62), that is, the second day after his death and burial, in order to prevent his resurrection "on the third day" (27:63–64), the two Marys come to see the tomb "after the Sabbath, as the first day of the week was dawning" (28:1a), that is, on the crucial "third day" after Jesus' death and burial, the day of his promised resurrection (16:21; 17:22–23; 20:17–19).

The two women come to see the tomb (28:1b). The positive orientation of the two Marys to the "tomb" of Jesus sharply conflicts with the negative posture of the Jewish leaders. The Jewish leaders "went" (*poreuthentes*) and secured the "tomb" (*taphon*) by sealing the stone with the guard (27:66), thus employing their authority in an attempt to prevent Jesus' resurrection. But the faithful women "came" (*ēlthen*) merely to "see" the "tomb" (*taphon*) (28:1b), thus placing themselves in a favorable position to witness the revelation of Jesus' promised resurrection through God's power. The reader sees in the two faithful Marys, then, a positive model of the proper orientation toward the tomb of Jesus in order to experience his resurrection, in contrast to the negative model of the faithless Jewish leaders and their futile action.

But their coming to see the tomb (28:1) also develops the passive sitting in the previous a scene (27:61). First, that the two Marys explicitly "came" marks a progression to a more active posture. Second, that they came precisely to "see" the "tomb" indicates their role as potential witnesses of the expected resurrection of Jesus. This is the third in the series of a scenes portraying the faithful presence and witness of Galilean women as substitutes for the absent disciples. This sequence of scenes assures the reader that there were reliable and continuous witnesses from Galilee to Jesus' death (27:55–56) and his burial (27:61), which enabled them to become reliable witnesses to the revelation of his resurrection.

An Angel Rolls Back the Stone, and the Fearful Guards Become as If Dead (b^3 28:2–4)

> [2]And behold, there was a great earthquake; for an angel of the Lord descended from heaven, approached, rolled back the stone, and sat upon it. [3]His appearance was like lightning and his clothing white as snow. [4]The guards were shaken with fear of him and became as if dead.

An angel rolls back the stone from the tomb (28:2–3). The angel rolling back the stone of the tomb so that the fearful guards become as if dead (28:2–4) not only contrasts with the previous a scene of the two Marys coming to see the tomb (28:1) but also develops the theme of authority over the dead body of Jesus in the previous b scene of the Jewish leaders sealing the stone of the tomb with the guard (27:62–66).

These verses present a dramatic reversal. In the first b scene Joseph of Arimathea "rolled" (*proskylisas*) a huge "stone" (*lithon*) across the entrance of the tomb (27:60). In the second b scene (27:66), the Jewish leaders' sealed the "stone" (*lithon*) with the guard. Here an "angel of the Lord" came down from heaven and "rolled back" (*apekylisen*) the "stone" (*lithon*). The angel then "sat upon it" (28:2), thus illustrating the triumph of God's power over the "stone" sealed by the futile, human power of the Jewish leaders.[8] The "earthquake" (see also 27:51) that accompanied the descent of the angel (28:2) and his "appearance" "like lightning" and "clothing" "white as snow" (28:3; see 17:2) emphasize the awesome character of the angel as an agent of God.

The guards are afraid and become as if dead (28:4). In striking contrast to the two Marys, whose coming "to see the tomb" (28:1) placed them in a position of reliable witness in the previous a scene, "the guards," whom the Jewish leaders have placed in the negative position of sealing the stone of the "tomb" in an effort to block Jesus' resurrection (27:66), are "shaken with fear" and "become as if dead" (28:4) when an angel spectacularly rolls back the stone of the tomb they are guarding (28:2). Ironically those guarding Jesus' tomb to prevent the proclamation that "he has been raised from the dead" (*nekrōn*, 27:64) themselves become "as if dead" (*nekroi*). The fearful and dead-like posture of those who were guarding the tomb contrasts with the receptive posture of the women who have come not to guard but simply to "see" the tomb. As the guards of the tomb are overwhelmed with fear and become "as if dead" in response to the angel of the Lord (28:4), the reader begins to realize the vast superiority of God's power to overcome any authority that would prevent the proclamation of Jesus' resurrection.

The Authority of the Risen Jesus Prevails (Matt 28:5–20)

The Women Are Sent to the Disciples by the Angel and the Risen Jesus (a[4] 28:5–10)

> [5]Then the angel said to the women, "You need not be afraid, for I know that you are seeking Jesus the crucified one. [6]He is not here, for he has been raised just as he said. Come and see the place where he lay. [7]Then go quickly and tell his disciples, 'He has been raised from the dead, and behold, he is going before you to Galilee; there you will see him.' Behold, I have told you."
>
> [8]Then going away quickly from the tomb with fear and great joy, they ran to announce it to his disciples. [9]And behold, Jesus met them, saying, "Hail!" They approached, embraced his feet and worshiped him. [10]Then Jesus said to them, "Go and announce to my brothers to go to Galilee, and there they will see me."

The angel sends the women to the disciples (28:5–7). The women being sent to the disciples by the angel and the risen Jesus (28:5–10) not only contrasts with the previous b scene of the guards being overcome with fear and becoming as if dead when the angel rolls back the stone of the tomb (28:2–4) but also advances the theme of the women's faithful presence and witness in the previous a scene of their coming to see the tomb (28:1).

In direct contrast to the guards, who were shaken "because of fear" (*apo de tou phobou*) of the angel, the same angel assures the women, "You need not be afraid" (*mē phobeisthe hymeis*), with the explicit expression of the personal pronoun *you* (*hymeis*) emphasizing the contrast between the women and the guards. The women need not be afraid "because" (*gar*) the angel, in his divine authority, "knows" that they are "seeking Jesus the crucified one" (28:5). That the women are seeking Jesus as "the one who has been and still is [they think] crucified" (*estaurōmenon*, perfect tense), then, privileges them to receive the angel's revelation that Jesus is no longer crucified but has been raised from the dead (28:6–7). The guards, by contrast, who have been stationed at the tomb by the Jewish leaders to keep Jesus as the "crucified one" within the realm of the dead (27:63–66), themselves become "as if dead" before God's angel (28:4). The reader thus views the women as specially authorized witnesses of the message of Jesus' resurrection over and against the "dead-like" guards.

This fourth a scene (28:5–10) stands in contrast not only with the previous third b scene (28:2–4) but also with the second b scene (27:62–66). The angel's divine revelation to the women that Jesus has been raised "just as he said" (*kathōs eipen*) (28:6) refutes the Jewish leaders' designation of Jesus as "this imposter" because "he said" (*eipen*) while still alive that "after three days I will be raised up" (27:63). That Jesus has been raised "just as he said" vindicates him against the charge that he is an "imposter" who falsely "said" he would be raised. Furthermore, the authoritative "telling" of the message of the resurrection by Jesus, the angel, and the women contradicts the ridiculous conjecture of the chief priests and Pharisees that the proclamation of Jesus' resurrection would be based on a fraudulent "telling" of it by the disciples who stole the body:

> Lest his disciples come and steal him and *tell* [*eipōsin*] the people, "He has been raised from the dead." (27:64)
> "He has been raised just as he *said* [*eipen*]." (28:6)
> "Go quickly and *tell* [*eipate*] his disciples, 'He has been raised from the dead.'" (28:7)
> "Behold, I have *told* [*eipon*] you." (28:7)

The women's commission to "tell" the disciples the message that "he has been raised from the dead" (*ēgerthē apo tōn nekrōn*) (28:7) reveals as false the Jewish leaders' charge that the disciples would deceptively "tell" the people that "he has been raised from the dead" (*ēgerthē apo tōn nekrōn*), after they had stolen the body (27:64). The women's "telling" is based upon the divine authority of the angel's "telling" ("behold, I have told you," 28:7), which in turn has confirmed the authority of Jesus' "telling" of his resurrection ("he has been raised just as he said," 28:6). This powerful contradiction equips the reader with the truth of the disciples' reception of the women's divinely authorized and previously promised message of Jesus' resurrection in order to overcome the false claim that the message of Jesus' resurrection originated from deception.

But the women being sent to the disciples by the angel and the risen Jesus (28:5–10) also develop the previous a scene of the women coming to see the tomb (28:1). The angel's making known that the women are "seeking Jesus the crucified one" (28:5) develops the motivation for their coming to see the tomb. That the women are seeking the crucified one recalls the women's witnessing of Jesus' death by crucifixion in the first a scene (27:55–56), further indicating that it is their witnessing of the reality of Jesus' death and burial (27:61) that qualifies them to be reliable witnesses of the message of Jesus' resurrection. The angel's invitation for the women to "come and see the place where he lay" (28:6) transforms the focus of their coming to see the tomb. The women who have "come" (*ēlthen*) expressly "to see" (*theōrēsai*) the tomb of the crucified Jesus are now beckoned by God's angel to "come" (*deute*) and "see" (*idete*) that the tomb is now empty, as proof that the crucified one "is not here" but "has been raised just as he said" (28:6).

Furthermore, the tension that was aroused by the women's passivity at Jesus' death (27:55–56) and burial (27:61), and that began to receive resolution in the active "coming" of the women to see the tomb (28:1), is now further resolved and transformed. The angel commissions the women with the divinely authorized activity of "going" and "telling" the disciples that Jesus "has been raised from the dead" and that, in fulfillment of his previous promise (26:32), he is going before them to Galilee where they will see him (28:7). As substitutes for the disciples who have been absent, the faithful Galilean women serve as the reliable intermediaries who are to link the disciples with the reality of Jesus' death, burial, and resurrection. Empowered by the divine authority of the angel, the previously passive women actively begin to fulfill their role as authentic messengers of Jesus' resurrection.

The risen Jesus encounters the women on their way (28:8–10). Quickly "going away" from the tomb,[9] with fear and great joy the women "ran to announce" the angel's message to the disciples (28:8). When the risen Jesus encounters the women on their way to the disciples, the earlier tension involving the women's lack of response to the death of Jesus (27:55–56), which stood in sharp contrast to the confession of his divine sonship by the centurion and those with him (27:54), is dramatically resolved. After the women are greeted by the risen Jesus, they "approached, embraced his feet and worshiped him" (28:9). The earlier exuberant confession by the newly converted gentile soldiers that the dead Jesus "was truly the Son of God" (27:54) is now complemented by this reverent homage toward Jesus on the part of these longtime Jewish followers, the Galilean women, who have patiently witnessed not only the death but also the burial, the angel of the Lord, the empty tomb, and now the risen Jesus himself.

After eliminating their fear, the risen Jesus reinforces the commission of these faithful women followers to direct the disciples, as "my brothers," back to Galilee in order to see him (28:10). That Jesus refers to his disciples as "my brothers" (*adelphois mou*) underlines the important role the faithful women are to play in the reconciliation of the absent disciples to their "brotherly" fellowship with Jesus in Galilee. Thus the women assure the reader not only of the reliable transmission of the true message of Jesus' resurrection to his absent disciples but also of their reunion with their risen master.

The Chief Priests and Elders Bribe the Guards to Say That the Disciples Stole the Body of Jesus (b^4 28:11–15)

> [11]While they were going, behold, some of the guard went into the city and announced to the chief priests all that had happened. [12]Then assembling with the elders and taking counsel, they gave plenty of silver pieces to the soldiers, [13]saying, "Tell that his disciples came at night and stole him while we were asleep. [14]And if this is heard by the governor, we will persuade him and keep you out of trouble." [15]Taking the silver pieces, they did as they were taught. And this story has circulated among the Jews until the present day.

Jewish leaders bribe the guard to spread deception (28:11–14). The chief priests and elders bribing the guards to say that the disciples stole the body of Jesus (28:11–15) not only contradict the previous a scene of the women being sent to the disciples by the angel and the risen Jesus (28:5–10) but also develop the theme of the previous b scene (28:2–4)—the futile attempt of the Jewish leaders to prevent the proclamation of Jesus' resurrection.

In contrast to the women of the previous a scene, who are now on their way (28:11) to "announce" (*apaggeilai*, 28:8; *apaggeilate*, 28:10) to the disciples that Jesus has been raised and that they are to go "to Galilee" to see him, some of the "guard" who were at the tomb (see 27:66) went "into the city" and "announced" (*apēggeilan*) to the chief priests all that had happened (28:11). The focus "to Galilee" (28:8, 10) as the place for the disciples to see and be reconciled with the risen Jesus is now contrasted with a focus "into the city" (28:11) of Jerusalem, where the Jewish leaders plan to prevent the proclamation of Jesus' resurrection. And the "announcing" of Jesus' resurrection by the women commissioned by the angel and the risen Jesus (28:5–10) now serves as a foil for the "announcing" of "all that had happened" by the guards to those who had commissioned them to guard the tomb to prevent the proclamation of Jesus' resurrection.

After the chief priests have heard the report by the guard of "all that had happened" (28:11), meaning the opening of the empty tomb (28:2) despite their attempt to keep it closed (27:66), they take counsel with the elders and through bribery commission the soldiers to "tell" that his disciples stole the body of Jesus from the tomb (28:12–13). Their deceitful commissioning clearly contradicts the angel's commissioning of the women:

> "Tell [*eipate*] his disciples that he has been raised from the dead." (28:7)
> "Tell [*eipate*] that his disciples came at night and stole him." (28:13)

For the reader, however, who knows that the disciples have been absent throughout the events of Jesus' death and burial, so that they must be informed by the women about his resurrection (28:8–10), the Jewish leaders' commissioning of the soldiers with a counter interpretation of the empty tomb emerges as an absurdity.

But this b scene of the chief priests and elders bribing the guards also advances the theme of the futile attempt of the Jewish leaders to prevent the proclamation of Jesus' resurrection in the previous b scene involving the guards of the tomb (28:2–4). After the chief priests learned "all that had happened" (28:11)—that their attempt to block the resurrection of Jesus by sealing the tomb had been thwarted (27:66)—they conferred with the elders (28:12) and concocted a false interpretation of the empty tomb. Through bribery the Jewish leaders persuaded the soldiers to distort the truth of "all that had happened" in the event revealing the empty tomb (28:2–4) into a blatant lie. Their deceit in urging the soldiers to say that the disciples stole Jesus from the tomb "while we were asleep" (28:13) defiantly contradicts the truth known by the reader—namely, that those guarding the tomb had actually become "as if dead," shaken by fear of the angel who revealed the tomb as empty (28:4).

Ironically the Jewish leaders, who were earlier trying to prevent a deceptive proclamation of the resurrection based on the promise of Jesus as this "deceiver" (27:63) in the b scene of 27:62–66, now become perpetrators of the very deception they were attempting to avert! Their concern to avoid the deception of the disciples' theft of Jesus from the tomb and the proclamation of a false message of his resurrection (27:64) now becomes their own deception:

> "Lest his disciples [*hoi mathētai autou*] come [*elthontes*] and steal him [*klepsōsin autou*]" (27:64)
>
> "Tell that his disciples [*hoi mathētai autou*] came [*elthontes*] at night and stole him [*eklepsan auton*]" (28:13)

They feared that "this last deception" (*planē*) of a false proclamation of Jesus' resurrection by his disciples "would be worse than the first" (27:64), the deception of the prediction of it by this "deceiver" (*planos*) (27:63). But the reader now experiences the ironic reversal that this last "deception" by the Jewish leaders involving their own false interpretation of Jesus' resurrection is worse than their own first "deception" (*dolos*, 26:4) in putting him to death. The Jewish leaders add to the shame of their deceit as they accept full responsibility for it. They assure the soldiers that they will persuade the Roman governor to keep them out of trouble (28:14).

The guards' false story continues among the Jews (28:15). As they accept the bribe of silver pieces and do "as they were taught," the soldiers emerge as indoctrinated puppets of the deceitful Jewish authorities, who are ultimately responsible for the tragedy of "this story"—the false interpretation of Jesus' resurrection—being circulated among the Jews until the present day (28:15). The reader must now reckon with the tragic deception "until the present day" of this counterproclamation of Jesus' resurrection, knowing that it is based upon the absurdity of the theft of Jesus by the disciples who have been absent throughout and who themselves learn of the resurrection only through the women. The theme of the b scenes (27:57–60, 62–66; 28:2–4, 11–15)—the futile and fraudulent attempts by the Jewish leaders to prevent faith in the risen Jesus—has now reached its climax.

In Galilee the Eleven Disciples See the Risen Jesus and Are Sent to Make Disciples of All Peoples (a[5] 28:16–20)

> [16]The eleven disciples went to Galilee, to the mountain to which Jesus
> has ordered them. [17]When they saw him, they worshiped, but some
> doubted. [18]Then Jesus approached and said to them, "All authority in
> heaven and on earth has been given to me. [19]Go, therefore, and make
> disciples of all peoples, baptizing them in the name of the Father, and of

> the Son, and of the Holy Spirit, [20]teaching them to observe all that I have commanded you. And behold, I am with you all days until the end of the age."

Disciples worship the risen Jesus in Galilee (28:16–17). The eleven disciples seeing the risen Jesus and being sent by him to make disciples of all peoples (28:16–20) not only contrast with the previous b scene of the Jewish leaders bribing the soldiers to say that the disciples stole Jesus' body (28:11–15) but also develop the theme of the reliable witnessing of the women in the previous a scene (28:5–10).

In contradiction to the Jewish leaders' allegation that "his disciples" came and stole Jesus' body from the tomb in the previous b scene (28:13), the "eleven disciples" actually "went to Galilee, to the mountain to which Jesus had ordered them" (28:16).[10] Subordinate to the authentic authority of Jesus, the eleven disciples, who returned "to Galilee" precisely "to the mountain" to which Jesus had "ordered" them, stand in contrast to "some of the guard," who returned "to the city" of Jerusalem to report on the tomb as subordinates to the deceitful authority of the Jewish leaders (28:11).

That "some"[11] of the disciples "doubted" (*edistasan*) when they "saw" and "worshiped" the risen Jesus (28:17) expresses the attitude of "little faith" (*oligopistos*, 6:30; 8:26; 14:31; 16:8; 17:20) that characterizes the disciples in Matthew and that is oriented to an increase in faith through a deeper experience of Jesus' divine power.[12] This salutary "doubt" on the part of some of the disciples before the risen Jesus contrasts sharply with the lack of any such doubt regarding the spreading of a false interpretation of the empty tomb on the part of the faithless characters in the previous b scene (28:11–15). The "Jews" among whom the false story about the empty tomb has circulated until the present day (28:15) apparently do not question its obvious contradiction, that if the soldiers were asleep when the disciples stole the body (28:13), how could they know it? Despite the thwarting by a superior power of their attempt to keep the tomb closed (27:66; 28:2–4, 11), the Jewish leaders do not hesitate to continue to oppose this power by devising a further deception against the resurrection (28:12–14). And the soldiers, although they were present at the dramatic opening of the empty tomb by the angel (28:2–4), demonstrate no doubt in accepting the bribe and instructions of the Jewish leaders to undermine the proclamation of Jesus' resurrection (28:12–15).

But the eleven disciples' being commissioned by the risen Jesus to make disciples of all peoples (28:16–20) also advances the theme of the faithful witnessing of the women being sent to the disciples by the angel and the risen Jesus in the previous a scene (28:5–10). That the eleven disciples went "to Galilee" (28:16) fulfills the instructions given the women by both the angel and Jesus that the disciples were to go "to Galilee" (28:7, 10) in order to see and be reconciled with the risen Jesus, as he had promised (26:32). The women, as substitutes for the disciples, have successfully executed their role of linking the absent disciples to the death, burial, and resurrection of Jesus.

The return of the disciples to Galilee indicates their reconciliation to their master as his "brothers" (28:10), after they had been absent (26:31, 56) throughout the events of his death and burial. When the disciples "saw" (*idontes*) the risen Jesus on the mountain in Galilee (28:17), the promise by both the angel and Jesus that they would "see" (*opsesthe*, 28:7; *opsontai*, 28:10) him there is fulfilled. That the disciples "worshiped" (*prosekynēsan*) the risen Jesus when they saw him (28:17) complements the women who likewise "worshiped" (*prosekynēsan*) him when he met them (28:9).

Jesus empowers the making of future disciples (28:18–20). That Jesus "has been given" (*edothē*) by God (divine passive) "all power/authority" (*pasa exousia*) in heaven and on earth (28:18) surpasses the power of the money the Jewish leaders "gave" (*edōkan*) to the soldiers as a bribe, authorizing them to spread a false proclamation against Jesus' resurrection (28:12–13). Likewise, the share in this absolute authority that the disciples receive as Jesus empowers them "to make disciples of all peoples" by baptizing and teaching (28:19–20) far exceeds the authority the soldiers receive from the Jewish leaders to prevent the making of disciples of the risen Jesus when they take their money (28:15).

The universal authority with which Jesus empowers his disciples to make disciples of "all peoples" (*panta ta ethnē*) (28:19) counters, embraces, and exceeds the limited authority of the Jewish leaders to circulate the false story regarding Jesus' resurrection only "among the Jews" (*para Ioudaiois*) (28:15).[13] The universal "teaching" (*didaskontes*) by the disciples to "all" peoples of "all" that Jesus had commanded them (28:20) overpowers the deceitful "teaching" of the bribed soldiers, who did as they were "taught" (*edidachthēsan*) by the Jewish leaders (28:15). Jesus' authoritative promise of abiding presence and protection of his disciples through his words, "behold, I am with you all days until the end of the age" (28:20), excels the Jewish leaders' limited promise to protect the bribed soldiers from the Roman governor (28:14).[14] And finally, Jesus' powerful promise to remain with his disciples "all days" (*pasas tas hēmeras*) until the end of the age (28:20) transcends the circulation among the Jews of the false story about the risen Jesus "until the present day" (*mechri tēs sēmeron* [*hēmeras*], 28:15).

Through the progressive experience of all of these contrasts, the reader, in identifying with the disciples, is called to an authentic faith in the absolute authority of the risen Jesus. Through this faith the reader is empowered with the superior authority of the risen Jesus to prevail effectively over the inferior, fraudulent authority that would prevent belief in the risen Jesus. With Jesus' promise of his abiding authority, the reader is equipped to predominate for "all days until the end of the age" (28:20) over the unbelief that persists only "until the present day" (28:15). The reader is thus invited to complete the disciples' mission to make disciples of all peoples (28:19) in order ultimately to eliminate the unbelief based on the false story of Jesus' resurrection circulated among the Jews (28:15).

The commission of the risen Jesus to the disciples far expands that given the women in the previous a scene (28:5–10). Whereas he commanded the women to direct the disciples to Galilee to see him and thus serve as the connecting link between them and his death, burial, and resurrection, he now commands the disciples to make disciples of all peoples (28:19) by baptizing them and teaching them all he taught (28:20), so that they are empowered to serve as the authoritative link between all peoples and the teaching, death, burial, and resurrection of Jesus. Because the witness of the women has linked the disciples to the death of Jesus (27:55–56), the universal mission of the disciples to make disciples will expand to "all peoples" the climactic confession of faith in Jesus' divine sonship by the gentile soldiers (27:54).

This final a scene, then, assures the reader of a reliable connection from the Gentiles' confession of faith at the death of Jesus (27:54) to the worship of the women (28:9) and of the disciples (28:17) to the making of all peoples into believing disciples of the risen Jesus (28:19). Through this completed sequence of a scenes (27:55–56, 61; 28:1, 5–10, 16–20) the reader has experienced a progressive witnessing to the events of Jesus' death, burial, empty tomb, and resurrection, which culminates in authentic faith in the divine authority of the Jesus who was crucified but is now risen. Through this faith the reader is empowered by the risen Jesus to continue the universal mission of the disciples to make disciples of all peoples.

Summary

This final sequence of scenes in Matthew's Gospel takes the reader through a progressive interchange of sharply opposing themes. Through the progression of a scenes (27:55–56, 61; 28:1, 5–10, 16–20) the reader experiences the continuity of reliable witnesses from the death to the resurrection of Jesus, culminating in authentic faith in and empowerment by the risen Lord. But through the alternating progression of b scenes (27:57–60, 62–66; 28:2–4, 11–15) the reader experiences the contrasting constancy of futile and fraudulent attempts to prevent faith in the risen Jesus.

Despite the departure of the rich disciple after he officially buried Jesus, the scenes of the faithful and continuous witnessing of the Galilean women as substitutes for the absent disciples at Jesus' death and burial prepare the reader for authentic faith in the risen Jesus. The attempt of the faithless Jewish leaders to use their power and authority to keep Jesus' tomb closed is rendered futile by the divinely authoritative angel who opens it. The faithful women who come to see the tomb, by contrast, portray for the reader a positive stance open to resurrection faith. And although the Jewish leaders have used their fraudulent power and authority to spread a false interpretation of Jesus' resurrection, the angel and the risen Jesus bring the women and the disciples to authentic faith in the risen Jesus, who grants his disciples and the reader his abiding divine power and authority to make disciples of all peoples.

The positive experience of the a scenes guides and equips the reader to confront and overcome the negative experience of the b scenes. In order to prevail over the giving and receiving of powerless and fraudulent authority by those who would prevent faith in and proclamation of the risen Jesus, the reader, after being brought to authentic faith in the crucified but now risen Jesus, is invited to receive and give the true and powerful authority of the risen Jesus to all peoples. With the promise of the risen Jesus' authoritative power and presence "for all days until the end of the age," the reader is equipped to eliminate the continuing lack of faith based on futile power and fraudulent authority "until the present day."

NOTES

1. In Matthew the term *disciple* (*mathētēs*) is reserved for certain male followers of Jesus, so that the women followers function here as substitute disciples. As J. C. Anderson ("Matthew: Gender and Reading," *The Bible and Feminist Hermeneutics*, Semeia 28, ed. M. A. Tolbert [Chico: Scholars, 1983] 3–27) notes, "The women at the cross and tomb [27:55–56, 61; 28:1–10] serve as foils for the disciples and play important roles the disciples should have played. Gender

seems to prevent their identification as disciples. They are an auxiliary group which can conveniently stand in for the disciples" (17, 20).

2. "Who also had become a disciple" (*hos kai autos emathēteuthē*, 27:57) means that Joseph became a disciple in addition to being rich, rather than he became a disciple in addition to the women, who were disciples. See Anderson, "Matthew," 18–20.

3. A literary criterion that justifies treating 27:57–60 as a scene in itself and separate from 27:61 is provide by the inclusion formed by the explicit notices of Joseph's entrance into and exit from the narrative: he "came" (*ēlthen*) in 27:57 and he "departed" (*apēlthen*) in 27:60.

Neither Mark nor Luke includes the explicit notice of Joseph's "departure" from the burial scene.

4. Matthew 27:61 begins a noteworthy shift in the Greek terms used to express "tomb" in the events concluding the Gospel. In 27:60 Joseph laid Jesus' body in his new "tomb," *mnēmeiō*, and rolled a huge stone across the entrance of the "tomb," *mnēmeiou*, but in 27:61 the women sit facing the "tomb," *taphou*. Although the terms *mnēmeion* and *taphos* appear to be synonymous words for "tomb" in the previous narrative (see 23:29), they seem to have distinctive functions in the account of the death-burial-resurrection. When the focus is away from "tombs," both those of the "saints" (27:52–53) and that of Jesus (27:60; 28:8), the word *mnēmeion* is employed; but when the focus is concentrated toward the "tomb" of Jesus as the locus of his anticipated resurrection (27:61, 64, 66; 28:1), the term *taphos* is used.

5. The "mother" of the "sons of Zebedee" (27:56), two male disciples, is no longer mentioned.

6. "Pharisees" were present when Jesus indirectly referred to his resurrection through the "sign of Jonah," who was in the belly of the whale for "three days and three nights" before being rescued, just as Jesus will be in the heart of the earth for "three days and three nights" before being raised (12:38–40).

7. M. Zerwick and M. Grosvenor, *A Grammatical Analysis of the Greek New Testament* (Rome: Biblical Institute, 1974, 1979) 1.97.

8. That the "seating" image of the angel who "sat upon it (the stone)" (*ekathēto epanō autou*, 28:2) indicates God's total power over the "stone" of the tomb is enhanced by the similar use of this image to express God's sovereign rule in the words of Jesus in 23:22: "One who swears by heaven swears by the throne of God and by him who is seated on it" (*kathēmenō epanō autou*).

9. Now that the narrative focus is once again away from the "tomb," the word *mnēmeion* is again used for "tomb" (see also 27:52–53, 60) in contrast to the term *taphos*, used when the focus is toward the tomb (27:61, 64, 66; 28:1).

10. The mention of "eleven" disciples recalls the defection of Judas, one of the "Twelve" (10:1–4; 26:14, 47), whose betrayal of Jesus (26:14–16, 20–25, 46–50; 27:3–10) was part of the Jewish leaders' "deceit" in putting Jesus to death (26:4).

11. On the controversy of whether to translate *hoi de* in 28:17 as "all" or

"some" of the disciples, we follow the reasoning of P. W. van der Horst, "Once More: The Translation of *hoi de* in Matthew 28.17," *JSNT* 27 (1986) 27–30, who translates: "When they saw him, they worshipped him, but some of them doubted."

12. The same verb for "doubt" (*distazō*) is closely combined with the theme of "little faith" in Jesus' question to Peter in 14:31, after he failed to walk across the water: "O man of little faith [*oligopiste*], why did you doubt [*edistasas*]?" Peter's "little faith" and "doubt" afforded him a deeper experience of Jesus' absolute power to save, calling him to a greater faith. See J. P. Heil, *Jesus Walking on the Sea: Meaning and Gospel Functions of Matt 14:22–33, Mark 6:45–52 and John 6:15b–21*, AnBib 87 (Rome: Biblical Institute, 1981) 63–64.

13. We understand "all peoples" (*panta ta ethnē*) to include the Jewish people.

14. See "Jesus as God-With-Us" in chap. 1.

CHAPTER 5

Conclusion

What is the significance of this narrative-critical, reader-response approach to Matthew's story of the passion, death, and resurrection of Jesus? It enables us, the readers of today, to experience the dynamic process of communication involved in the intricate structures formed by these Matthean scenes. Matthew does not merely inform us about what happened, but summons us as his audience to respond actively to the unfolding of these events, allowing their intense interplay to absorb us. As we encounter the conflicts of the contrasting themes that comprise this human and divine drama, we are better equipped to deal with the conflict between the human and the divine in our own lives.

As we move through Matthew 26:1–56, the disciples and the enemies of Jesus remind us of our potential, despite our best intentions, likewise to oppose and abandon the plan of God revealed by Jesus. But our identification with Jesus assures us that the intimate bond he has established with his disciples and us through his unique prayerful union with the Father will triumph over all human failure (chapter 2).

Our reading of Matthew 26:57—27:54 invites us to overcome our difficulties in following Jesus as God's suffering just one by imitating the examples of conversion provided by those who withdraw from the unjust opposition surrounding the death imposed upon him. By emulating the inspiring model of Jesus as the innocently suffering just one, who, through complete trust in God, patiently endures rejection and death from his own people, we can withstand our own suffering and rejection as Christians (chapter 3).

In Matthew 27:55—28:20 the continuity of reliable witnesses from the death to the resurrection of Jesus leads us to authentic faith in the crucified but now risen Lord. This faith enables us to prevail over the exercise of fraudulent authority by those who would prevent faith in and proclamation of the risen Jesus. We are assured that the risen Lord continuously empowers us with his divine authority to make true believers of all peoples (chapter 4).

Through our narrative-critical reading of Matthew's presentation of the death and resurrection of Jesus we not only deepen our appreciation of what it communicates to us but are prepared to fulfill our responsibility to communicate it to others.

Bibliography

Allison, D. C. "The Structure of the Sermon on the Mount." *JBL* 106 (1987) 423–45.

———. "Two Notes on a Key Text: Matthew 11:25–30." *JTS* 39 (1988) 477–85.

———. "Matthew 10:26–31 and the Problem of Evil." *St. Vladimir's Theological Quarterly* 32 (1988) 293–308.

Anderson, J. C. "Matthew: Gender and Reading." *The Bible and Feminist Hermeneutics*. Semeia 28. Ed. M. A. Tolbert. Chico: Scholars, 1983, 3–27.

———. "Matthew: Sermon and Story." SBLASP 27 (1988) 496–507.

Barta, K. A. "Mission in Matthew: The Second Discourse as Narrative." SBLASP 27 (1988) 527–35.

Bauer, D. R. *The Structure of Matthew's Gospel: A Study in Literary Design*. JSNTSup 31. Sheffield: Almond, 1988.

Beare, F. W. *The Gospel According to Matthew: Translation, Introduction, and Commentary*. San Francisco: Harper & Row, 1981.

Black, C. C. "Depth of Characterization and Degrees of Faith in Matthew." SBLASP 28 (1989) 604–23.

Bloem, H. *Die Ostererzählung des Matthäus: Aufbau und Aussage von Mt 27,57—28,20*. Zeist: no publisher, 1987.

Bolognesi, P. "Matteo 28,16–20 e la sua struttura." *BeO* 30 (1988) 129–37.

Brown, R. E. *The Birth of the Messiah*. Garden City: Doubleday, 1977.

Burchard, C. "Senfkorn, Sauerteig, Schatz und Perle in Matthäus 13." SUNT 13 (1988) 5–35.

Burnett, F. W. "Characterization in Matthew: Reader Construction of the Disciple Peter." *McKendree Pastoral Review* 4 (1987) 13–43.

———. "Characterization and Christology in Matthew: Jesus in the Gospel of Matthew." SBLASP 28 (1989) 588–603.

Calloud, J. "Entre les écritures et la violence: la passion du témoin." *RSR* 73 (1985) 111–28.

Caragounis, C. C. *The Son of Man: Vision and Interpretation*. WUNT 38. Tübingen: Mohr-Siebeck, 1986.

Charette, B. "A Harvest for the People? An Interpretation of Matthew 9.37f." *JSNT* 38 (1990) 29–35.

Cook, J. G. "The Sparrow's Fall in Mt 10:29b." *ZNW* 79 (1988) 138–44.

Cope, O. L. *Matthew: A Scribe Trained for the Kingdom of Heaven.* CBQMS 5. Washington: Catholic Biblical Association, 1976.

Crosby, M. H. *House of Disciples: Church, Economics, and Justice in Matthew.* Maryknoll, N.Y.: Orbis, 1988.

Davies, W. D. *The Setting of the Sermon on the Mount.* Cambridge: Cambridge University, 1966.

Davies, W. D., and D. C. Allison. *The Gospel According to Saint Matthew: Volume I: Introduction and Commentary on Matthew I–VII.* ICC. Edinburgh: T. & T. Clark, 1988.

De Boer, M. C. "Ten Thousand Talents? Matthew's Interpretation and Redaction of the Parable of the Unforgiving Servant (Matt 18:23–35)." *CBQ* 50 (1988) 214–32.

Delorme, J. "Sémiotique du récit de la Passion." *RSR* 73 (1985) 85–110.

Deutsch, C. "Wisdom in Matthew: Transformation of a Symbol." *NovT* 32 (1990) 13–47.

Donaldson, T. L. *Jesus on the Mountain: A Study in Matthean Theology.* JSNTSup 8. Sheffield: JSOT, 1985.

Doyle, B. R. "Matthew's Intention as Discerned by His Structure." *RB* 95 (1988) 34–54.

du Plessis, J. G. "Pragmatic Meaning in Matthew 13:1–23." *Neot* 21 (1987) 33–56.

Feldkämper, L. *Der betende Jesus als Heilsmittler nach Lukas.* Veröffentlichungen des Missionspriesterseminars St. Augustin bei Bonn 29. St. Augustin, West Germany: Steyler, 1978.

Fowler, R. M. "Who Is 'the Reader' in Reader Response Criticism?" *Reader Response Approaches to Biblical and Secular Texts.* Ed. R. Detweiler. Semeia 31. Decatur: Scholars, 1985, 5–23.

Freed, E. D. "The Women in Matthew's Genealogy." *JSNT* 29 (1987) 3–19.

Funk, R. W. *The Poetics of Biblical Narrative.* Sonoma: Polebridge, 1988.

Gaechter, P. *Das Matthäus Evangelium.* Innsbruck: Tyrolia, 1963.

Garland, D. E. "Matthew's Understanding of the Temple Tax (Matt 17:24–27)." SBLASP 26 (1987) 190–209.

Gerhardsson, B. *The Testing of God's Son (Matt 4:1–11 & Par).* ConBNT 2/1. Lund: Gleerup, 1966.

______. "Jesus livré et abandonné d'après la Passion selon Saint Matthieu." *RB* 76 (1969) 206–27.

Giblin, C. H. "Structural and Thematic Correlations in the Matthean Burial-Resurrection Narrative (Matt. xxvii. 57—xxviii. 20)." *NTS* 21 (1974–75) 406–20.

Gnilka, J. *Das Matthäusevangelium: Kommentar zu Kap. 1,1—13,58.* HTKNT 1/1. Freiburg/Basel/Vienna: Herder, 1986.

______. *Das Matthäusevangelium: Kommentar zu Kap. 14,1—28,20 und Einleitungsfragen.* HTKNT 1/2. Freiburg/Basel/Vienna: Herder, 1988.

Gnuse, R. "Dream Genre in the Matthean Infancy Narratives." *NovT* 32 (1990) 97–120.

Good, D. "The Verb *anachoreo* in Matthew's Gospel." *NovT* 32 (1990) 1–12.

Gundry, R. H. *The Use of the Old Testament in St. Matthew's Gospel.* NovTSup 18. Leiden: Brill, 1967.

———. *Matthew: A Commentary on His Literary and Theological Art.* Grand Rapids: Eerdmans, 1982.

Heil, J. P. "Significant Aspects of the Healing Miracles in Matthew." *CBQ* 41 (1979) 274–87.

———. *Jesus Walking on the Sea: Meaning and Gospel Functions of Matt 14:22–33, Mark 6:45–52 and John 6:15b-21.* AnBib 87. Rome: Biblical Institute, 1981.

———. "Reader-Response and the Irony of Jesus Before the Sanhedrin in Luke 22:66–71." *CBQ* 51 (1989) 271–84.

Hill, D. "Matthew 27,51–53 in the Theology of the Evangelist." *IBS* 7 (1985) 76–87.

———. "The Conclusion of Matthew's Gospel: Some Literary-Critical Observations." *IBS* 8 (1986) 54–63.

Horton, F. L. "Parenthetical Pregnancy: The Conception and Birth of Jesus in Matthew 1:18–25." SBLASP 26 (1987) 175–89.

Keegan, T. J. *Interpreting the Bible: A Popular Introduction to Biblical Hermeneutics.* New York/Mahwah N.J.: Paulist, 1985.

Kingsbury, J. D. "The Parable of the Wicked Husbandmen and the Secret of Jesus' Divine Sonship in Matthew." *JBL* 105 (1986) 643–55.

———. "The Developing Conflict between Jesus and the Jewish Leaders in Matthew's Gospel: A Literary-Critical Study." *CBQ* 49 (1987) 57–73.

———. "Reflections on 'the Reader' of Matthew's Gospel." *NTS* 34 (1988) 442–60.

———. *Matthew as Story.* 2d ed. Philadelphia: Fortress, 1988.

———. "Matthew." *The Books of the Bible.* Vol. II. *The Apocrypha and the New Testament.* Ed. B. W. Anderson. New York: Charles Scribner's Sons, 1989, 125–47.

Krentz, E. "Community and Character: Matthew's Vision of the Church." SBLASP 26 (1987) 565–73.

Lategan, B. C., and W. S. Vorster, eds. *Text and Reality. Aspects of Reference in Biblical Texts.* Atlanta: Scholars, 1985.

Lentzen-Deis, F. *Die Taufe Jesu nach den Synoptikern.* Frankfurter Theologische Studien 4. Frankfurt: Knecht, 1970.

———. "Passionsbericht als Handlungsmodell? Überlegungen zu Anstössen aus der 'pragmatischen' Sprachwissenschaft für die exegetischen Methoden." *Der Prozess gegen Jesus: Historische Rückfrage und theologische Deutung.* QD 112. Ed. K. Kertelge. Freiburg/Basel/Vienna: Herder, 1988, 191–232.

Luz, U. *Matthew 1–7: A Commentary.* Minneapolis: Augsburg, 1989.

Maisch, I. "Die österliche Dimension des Todes Jesu. Zur Osterverkündigung in Mt 27,51–54." *Auferstehung Jesu—Auferstehung der Christen: Deutungen des Osterglaubens.* QD 105. Ed. L. Oberlinner. Freiburg/Basel/Vienna: Herder, 1986, 96–123.

Marcus, J. "The Gates of Hades and the Keys of the Kingdom (Matt 16:18–19)." *CBQ* 50 (1988) 443–55.

Matera, F. J. "Matthew 27:11–54." *Int* 38 (1984) 55–59.

______. *Passion Narratives and Gospel Theologies: Interpreting the Synoptics Through Their Passion Stories.* Mahwah N.J.: Paulist, 1986.

______. "The Plot of Matthew's Gospel." *CBQ* 49 (1987) 233–53.

Meier, J. P. "Salvation-History in Matthew: In Search of a Starting Point." *CBQ* 37 (1975) 203–15.

______. *Law and History in Matthew's Gospel.* AnBib 71. Rome: Biblical Institute, 1976.

______. "Gentiles or Nations in Matt 28:19?" *CBQ* 39 (1977) 94–102.

______. *The Vision of Matthew: Christ, Church, and Morality in the First Gospel.* New York: Paulist, 1979.

______. *Matthew.* New Testament Message 3. Wilmington: Glazier, 1980.

______. "John the Baptist in Matthew's Gospel." *JBL* 99 (1980) 383–405.

Meyer, B. F. "Many (= All) Are Called, but Few (= Not All) Are Chosen." *NTS* 36 (1990) 89–97.

Moo, D. J. *The Old Testament in the Gospel Passion Narratives.* Sheffield: Almond, 1983.

Mowrey, R. L. "God, Lord, and Father: The Theology of the Gospel of Matthew." *BR* 33 (1988) 24–36.

______. "The Activity of God in the Gospel of Matthew." SBLASP 28 (1989) 400–411.

Neirynck, F. "*APO TOTE ERXATO* and the Structure of Matthew." *ETL* 64 (1988) 21–59.

Newman, B. M., and P. C. Stine, *A Translator's Handbook on the Gospel of Matthew.* New York: United Bible Societies, 1988.

Niedner, F. A. "Rereading Matthew on Jerusalem and Judaism." *BTB* 19 (1989) 43–47.

Nolan, B. M. *The Royal Son of God: The Christology of Matthew 1–2 in the Setting of the Gospel.* OBO 23. Göttingen: Vandenhoeck & Ruprecht, 1979.

Oberweis, M. "Beobachtungen zum AT-Gebrauch in der matthäischen Kindheitsgeschichte." *NTS* 35 (1989) 131–49.

Orton, D. E. *The Understanding Scribe: Matthew and the Apocalyptic Ideal.* JSNTSup 25. Sheffield: JSOT, 1989.

Pantle-Schieber, K. "Anmerkungen zur Auseinandersetzung von *ekklesia* und Judentum im Matthäusevangelium." *ZNW* 80 (1989) 145–62.

Patte, D. *The Gospel According to Matthew: A Structural Commentary on Matthew's Faith.* Philadelphia: Fortress, 1987.

Plank, K. A. *Paul and the Irony of Affliction.* Atlanta: Scholars, 1987.

Popkes, W. "Die Gerechtigkeitstradition im Matthäus-Evangelium." *ZNW* 80 (1989) 1–23.

Resseguie, J. L. "Reader-Response Criticism and the Synoptic Gospels." *JAAR* 52 (1984) 307–24.

Riebl, M. *Auferstehung Jesu in der Stunde seines Todes? Zur Botschaft von Mt 27,51b-53*. SBB 8. Stuttgart: Katholisches Bibelwerk, 1978.

Riekert, S.J.P.K. "The Narrative Coherence in Matthew 26–8." *Neot* 16 (1982) 118–36.

Sand, A. *Das Evangelium nach Matthäus*. RNT. Regensburg: Pustet, 1986.

Schenke, L., ed. *Studien zum Matthäusevangelium: Festschrift für Wilhelm Pesch*. SBS. Stuttgart: Katholisches Bibelwerk, 1988.

Scott, B. B. *Hear Then the Parable: A Commentary on the Parables of Jesus*. Minneapolis: Fortress, 1989.

Senior, D. *The Passion Narrative According to Matthew: A Redactional Study*. BETL 39. Leuven: Leuven University, 1975.

______. "The Death of Jesus and the Resurrection of the Holy Ones (Mt 27:51–53)." *CBQ* 38 (1976) 312–29.

______. *The Passion of Jesus in the Gospel of Matthew*. Wilmington: Glazier, 1985.

______. "Matthew's Special Material in the Passion Story: Implications for the Evangelist's Redactional Technique and Theological Perspective." *ETL* 63 (1987) 272–94.

Sim, D. C. "The Man Without the Wedding Garment (Matthew 22:11–13)." *HeyJ* 31 (1990) 165–78.

Snodgrass, K. "Matthew and the Law." SBLASP 27 (1988) 536–54.

Soares Prabhu, G. M. *The Formula Quotations in the Infancy Narrative of Matthew*. AnBib 63. Rome: Biblical Institute, 1976.

Staley, J. L. *The Print's First Kiss: A Rhetorical Investigation of the Implied Reader in the Fourth Gospel*. SBLDS 82. Atlanta: Scholars, 1988.

Stanton, G. N. "'Pray that your flight may not be in Winter or on a Sabbath' (Matthew 24.20)." *JSNT* 37 (1989) 17–30.

Stramare, T. "L'annunciazione a Giuseppe in Mt. 1,18–25: Analisi letteraria e significato teologico." *BeO* 31 (1989) 3–14.

Turiot, C. "Sémiotique et lisibilité du texte évangélique." *RSR* 73 (1985) 161–75.

van Aarde, A. G. "Resonance and Reception: Interpreting Mt 17:24–27 in Context." *Scriptura* 29 (1989) 1–12.

van Boxel, P. W. "You have heard that it was said." *Bijdr* 49 (1988) 362–77.

van der Horst, P. W. "Once More: The Translation of *hoi de* in Matthew 28.17." *JSNT* 27 (1986) 27–30.

Van Tilborg, S. *The Jewish Leaders in Matthew*. Leiden: Brill, 1972.

Verseput, D. J. *The Rejection of the Humble Messianic King: A Study of the Composition of Matthew 11–12*. Frankfurt am Main: Peter Lang, 1986.

______. "The Role and Meaning of the 'Son of God' Title in Matthew's Gospel." *NTS* 33 (1987) 532–56.

Via, D. O. "The Gospel of Matthew: Hypocrisy as Self-Deception." SBLASP 27 (1988) 508–16.

Viviano, B. T. "The Gospel According to Matthew." *The New Jerome Biblical*

Commentary. Ed. R. E. Brown, J. A. Fitzmyer, and R. E. Murphy. Englewood Cliffs, N.J.: Prentice-Hall, 1990, 630–74.

______. "The Genres of Matthew 1–2: Light from 1 Timothy 1:4." *RB* 97 (1990) 31–53.

Vorster, W. S. "The Reader in the Text: Narrative Material." *Reader Perspectives on the New Testament*. Ed. E. V. McKnight. Semeia 48. Atlanta: Scholars, 1989, 21–39.

Wilkins, M. J. *The Concept of Disciple in Matthew's Gospel*. NovTSup 59. Leiden: Brill, 1988.

Witherup, R. D. "The Death of Jesus and the Raising of the Saints: Matthew 27:51–54 in Context." SBLASP 26 (1987) 574–85.

Zerwick, M., and M. Grosvenor. *A Grammatical Analysis of the Greek New Testament*. 2 vols. Rome: Biblical Institute, 1974, 1979.

Scripture Index

Old Testament

New Testament